AF413299

WHAT YOU CAN DO ABOUT IT

TAKING REAL ACTION AGAINST CORRUPTION, RADICALISM, AND MORAL DECAY TO SAVE AMERICA

COL. ROBERT L. MANESS, RET.

"This excellent book by my friend, retired Air Force Colonel Rob Maness, comes a couple decades too late for me. I'm not sure whether I could've leveraged his vast experience as a strategist and a leader best as a commander myself, or a name partner at a firm, or even as political activist, but it's not too late for you to get the full benefit of the vast experience of this combat leader and graduate multiple multiple war colleges. And, as icing on the cake, it's entertaining. Doing something about it starts with you reading *What You Can Do About It*."

—Kurt Schlichter
Colonel, US Army (Ret.)
Senior Columnist, Townhall.com

"Rob Maness is exactly what he calls Charlie Kirk, the person to whom he dedicates his book—'a friend, a patriot, and a door-opener.' No one has helped STARRS (an organization I helped found to save our military from the Marxist march into our institutions) more than Rob. In this must read, Rob goes way beyond just describing the problem and the challenges conservatives are facing. He gives concrete recommendations on what the average American citizen can do to save our Republic. Read, heed, and join the fight! America is definitely worth saving!"

—Rod Bishop
Lt. Gen., USAF (Ret.)
Co-Founder, Director, Chairman Emeritus,
Stand Together Against Racism and Radicalism in the Services,
Inc. (STARRS.US)

"I finished *What You Can Do About It* on my flight back from Los Angeles—a book written by my former Commander, Colonel Rob Maness (ret). Like a true commander, he doesn't tolerate simply identifying the problem—he offers solutions (aka, 'courses of action' in the military). The book is a call to moral courage while counting the cost of following through on our convictions. I highly recommend!"

—Chris LaPack
Colonel, USAF

"Few Americans know more about what is truly at stake than Col. Rob Maness. Having served our nation in uniform and continuing to fight for our Republic at home, he offers *What You Can Do About It* as a loud call to action, urging those with a love of country in their hearts and the moral clarity to know what is right to stop being spectators to the world around them and instead make a difference in their communities, states, and nation."

—Cliff Maloney
CEO, Citizens Alliance
Co-Author, *Run Right: A Complete Election Playbook to Win*

"As one of the most powerful voices in the constitutional movement, Colonel Rob Maness intensifies his clarion call for liberty in his book, *What You Can Do About It*. His work arms everyday Americans not just with the knowledge required to fight back but with a framework for stopping the erosion of our nation's freedoms and values. Take the time to read this book and join in the fight to save America!"

—Robert A. Green, Jr.
Author, *Defending the Constitution Behind Enemy Lines: A Story of Hope for Those Who Love Liberty*

This book is dedicated to Charlie Kirk—a friend, a patriot, and a door-opener for so many of us who never would have considered there is a place for us, too, to do something about it.

Charlie, you will be sorely missed. May you rest in peace.

Till we meet again.

And we will.

Names: Maness, Robert, author.
Title: What you can do about it : taking real action against corruption, radicalism, and moral decay to save America / Robert Maness.
Description: Gulfport, MS : GatorPAC Direct Inc., [2026] | Includes bibliographical references.
Identifiers: ISBN: 9798995537403 (hardcover) | 9798995537410 (softcover) | 9798995537427 (ebook) | 9798995537434 (audiobook)
Subjects: LCSH: Political participation--United States. | Patriotism--United States. | Political parties--United States. | Political corruption--United States. | Radicalism--United States. | United States--Politics and government--21st century.
Classification: LCC: JK1764 .M36 2026 | DDC: 323.0420973--dc23

Contents

Foreword by Joshua Lisec

Charlie Kirk is how I met Rob Maness. Our mutual friend, journalist and veteran Navy intelligence officer Jack Posobiec, had invited me to join him for a panel discussion at Turning Point Action's America Fest (AmFest) 2024. Jack and I talked about public opinion manipulation, the necessity of amateur reporting, and the future of truth itself in a Left-wing-dominated, post-fact media world.

The broader context at the time was, of course, the recent victory of then-President-Elect Donald J. Trump and the greater work to be done by the Right to take back America—both top-down and bottom-up. We the people of principle must learn to wield power with righteousness and clarity. Principle alone is not enough, reminding us of Charlie's own Evangelical Christian faith and the teaching that "faith without works is dead" from James 2:17. Faith without works is dead; principle without power is doomed.

The bizarre and brutal election season that brought us multiple assassination attempts, politically motivated murder, and a literal palace coup had culminated in executive victory for the good guys. But that would not be enough. It will not be enough. There are works for each of us to do, and the complacency of celebration-basking would ensure we wouldn't do them.

Rob was in attendance that day at AmFest. I remember . . . outside, he came right up to Jack for a few words, after which Jack introduced us. We spoke books on the spot, Rob shared his desire to author one, and we connected later that night at a special Republican party event keynoted by Roger Stone. I'll admit . . . we didn't listen to Roger as much as we listened to each other. That marked a meeting of the minds—and soon-to-be-writing partners.

We finished this book together only days before the man who embodied the spirit of the movement—Turning Point founder Charlie Kirk—was brutally assassinated in front of his family, thousands of students, and in front of the entire world. So many cameras caught so many close-ups of his grisly end. Most of us wish we hadn't seen it. But we needed to. We needed to see what the Left is truly capable of—not in some far-away communist revolution of the distant past, but here in America in public in the current year. That's what time it is. Blood and gore are the hands of the clock.

Charlie's death became the turning point. As I write these very words, we are exactly one week out from the assassination. The killer is in custody, his network is under investigation, the so-called broader anti-fascist movement ("Antifa") in the United States has been designated domestic terrorism, and tens of thousands of grave-dancing leftists, liberals, and next-door-neighbor Democrats are losing their jobs, their homes, and their freedoms. Minutes before I wrote this paragraph, late-night host Jimmy Kimmel saw his national television show put on hiatus, after he falsely claimed that the openly-Left-wing shooter was in fact a Trump supporter.

For years, feckless conservatives cried hypocrite and whined, "What if the roles were reversed?!"

Now, they are.

In the days, hours, and even minutes after Charlie's death was announced to the gut-punched American public, I heard friends, clients, and allies all asking, "What can I do? What can I do now? What can I do right now to honor Charlie?"

There is something you can do about it—*What You Can Do About It.*

This very book, finished just prior to Charlie's martyrdom, answers these painful questions in advance. It cannot (just) be up to elected officials and law enforcement to seek justice, pursue righteousness, and honor the legacy of the fallen. It cannot (just) be up to election seasons every two and four years to put points on the board for the Right. And it cannot (just) be up to influencers, celebrities, and the donor class to make things happen the rest of the time.

We are all Charlie now. We are all drafted into a righteous war—not a literal war, mind you, where arms are taken up. After all, we the Right are the side of orderly justice, not blind rage and bloodthirsty hate. The aftermath of Charlie Kirk's assassination, where we witnessed nurses, school teachers, government workers, and more everyday citizens celebrate his slaughter . . . that is who *they* are. That is what *they* do. Not us.

When George Floyd overdosed, his supporters burned cities to the ground. When Charlie Kirk bled out on camera, his supporters prayed for his widow, his children, and his soul—and even, as no shock to Christians, for the soul of his killer.

We are not the same.

The energy Charlie's death unleashed, we must each commit to carrying forward now. If we don't, it will be lost. We cannot dishonor our slain friend. Charlie lived his life the American way. Let us do the same. Let us get involved. Do something right. Embrace faith, from which all else flows. And let us never surrender, never give up, and never quit the fight . . . fight . . . fight.

Every generation has its seventeen-year-olds who think they can change the world. Young Charlie thought he could. And he did.

He did.

Whether you're seventeen, thirty-seven, seventy-seven, or any age in between, younger, or older . . . you can, too. This is what it will take: *Know thyself.* Specifically, identify your strengths. Build them stronger. Be honest about your weaknesses. Fortify them. Learn more every day. Dedicate yourself to the cause, to *a* cause, to *any* cause that aligns with your values—one which you yourself are personally willing and able to cast a compelling vision for . . . for your fellow patriots to pick up and pass on.

Charlie showed the way.

Now it's your turn.

Rob Maness will take you from here.

For Charlie.

Joshua Lisec
September 17th, 2025

CHAPTER 1
Become Who You Are

It was a cold desert night on the Arabian Peninsula. Most people don't know how cold it gets in that part of the world. It's night and day, literally. You might feel like dressing for a tropical beach vacation when the sun rises; when it falls, it's freezing. But that night, I didn't feel the cold. I didn't feel anything. All that occupied my mind, my emotions, my whole word . . . was the mission.

Imagine a huge military airfield. It was even bigger than that. I stood on the parking ramp beneath my jet, preparing to launch on a specific, high-value target mission. This would ultimately become the modern equivalent of the maximum effort bomber operations you read about from World War II. And in that exact and precise moment, all geared up and ready for war, I fully realized how I had become a combat flying squadron commander—the most sought-after position of success in my profession of military aviation.

Just twenty-four hours earlier, the squadron I commanded, the 9th Expeditionary Bomb Squadron, had been settling into a routine combat operation from an island thousands of miles away. Out of the blue, after landing from my last combat sortie into Afghanistan, I was called to the command center. The briefing was simple and sobering: I was to immediately launch three B-1 bombers and lead them to a location on the Arabian Peninsula.

And now, it's go time. I stood on a darkened ramp, about to board my jet on that first combat mission to find and eliminate one of the two highest-value targets in the response to 9/11 and it hit me—I'd been entrusted not only with the mission but with the lives of the American service members who flew with me, together with all the maintenance and support personnel under my command. This trust came despite the fact that I'd always been told I didn't have what it took to be successful. Yet there I was.

Before boarding the aircraft, I spoke with my Senior Noncommissioned Officer, Master Sergeant Mike Miller. I reminded him (even though it really wasn't necessary because Mike was the best NCO I ever worked flying operations with) to take good care of our men and women—especially the bomb loaders and the fuels troops. This exchange was more than a one-time thing. Ours become a daily conversation, every day for two solid weeks. Eventually, exhaustion caught up with me; I'd have Mike physically lift me in and out of my ejection seat so I could continue flying missions.

When that fateful operation was completed, I asked Mike to take me to see the fuels airmen even though I was exhausted after my last mission. They were the hardest-working part of the team during that unbelievable operation. Most had worked twenty-four hours a day with little sleep for those two weeks. It was again the middle of the night. But when I arrived, the entire shop was there. Their normally white work coveralls were jet black. Even their skin was slick with fuel. They looked like coal miners.

I circled the room, shook each hand, and thanked them for their efforts. I expressed my sincere gratitude for their service to our great nation. And as I left to get briefed on our next mission phase, it hit me. Everything I had ever learned about leadership, responsibility, and resilience was being expressed, in that moment, right there in the sands of the Middle East.

The men and women of the 9th honored our unit by delivering combat capability under the most trying circumstances—without a single failure. I was awarded a Bronze Star Medal for superior combat leadership during the deployment. Truth be told, every one of them should have received one, too. They did receive special recognition with a Commander-in-Chief's Award, and one of our aircrews was awarded the LeMay Trophy for the most outstanding bomber crew in the entire United States Air Force that year.

And this story is but one from over forty years of work. I'm offering a peek into the ultimate success of someone who started at the lowest rank and rose, against the odds. That is the American way.

My high school guidance counselor once told me I wasn't college material. She added that I certainly wasn't qualified to be an officer in the military—even with above-average grades. I set out to prove her wrong. I didn't give myself a choice or an out. I come from a long line of American military volunteers that goes all the way back to July of 1775. I was raised to believe nothing is impossible. And my family was right. Nothing is.

My success wasn't typical for an Air Force officer. I had a lot going against me—previously enlisted, not part of the "in crowd," and lacking a legacy background, meaning multiple family members on both sides hail from the military officer corps. These days, such legacy appointments fill our academies. I didn't come from that. My parents weren't even high school graduates. And my granddad was a jack of all trades, as you had to be in those days to get by. He was a deputy sheriff who ran the local telephone exchange. He'd have his daughters climb the poles and literally cut off lines when people didn't pay their bills. On a job in the middle of the night, he got shot at by illegal moonshiners. On my dad's side were farmers. All sides were working folks. We worked, and we ate, like the Bible says. And we do it with pride in our heritage and honoring all the sacrifices made along the way so we have the privilege to do the same. We all are part of the great American story, and the next chapter is ours to tell. This, I understood from a tender age.

I distinctly remember standing on the courthouse steps in Jackson, Tennessee, when I was seven years old. That's in West Tennessee where the legendary pioneer-statesman-soldier David "Davy" Crockett was from. Crockett served in Congress twice and lost the second time chiefly because President Andrew Jackson—another Tennessee legend—didn't like that Crockett opposed his forced removal of Native Americans. The Trail of Tears—Crockett stood against it.

My Uncle "Buddy" (real name, Emmett) used to walk me around Jackson during our regular family visits. My dad was in the Air Force, but he made sure we spent at least four weeks a year in West Tennessee. He wanted us to learn about family and service, lost lessons for so many in the next generations. (You already see hints at why I felt called to write this book. And you, too, for why you're reading it.) Uncle Buddy didn't have kids of his own then, so he often took me under his wing.

On one particular trip, Uncle Buddy led me up the courthouse steps. The scene was classic Southern: courthouse in the middle, streets all around, storefronts lining the square. He pointed to a spot and said, "Roby, I want you to know that right here is where Davy Crockett said, 'Y'all can all go to hell—I'm going to Texas.'" That sticks with a kid. Of course I later learned, Crockett died defending Texans from the Mexican invasion at the Alamo. The more things change, the more they remain the same.

Davy Crockett, like so many legendary Americans, lives on as folk heroes tend to do because they were commoners with no wealth, particular genius, or aristocratic privileges. They were given no chance, so they *took it*. This is the first lesson I wish to impart to you, dear reader: The American way doesn't ask for permission. But when we're told we can't, shouldn't, or won't do something, we take that only one way: it's an invitation to winning.

The first time I was told I couldn't do something I wanted badly was by that guidance counselor. It stunned me. I had done well in school. I dreamed of becoming a fighter pilot—maybe even a Thunderbird pilot. I didn't achieve exactly that. I became a navigator and flew as a weapon systems officer. But I served as a flying squadron commander. I flew supersonic in big airplanes. I served my country far beyond what anyone expected of me, including myself.

As a kid, I was a severe introvert. Quiet at family gatherings. Quiet in class. Yet, I became a flying squadron commander, a vice wing commander, and eventually a wing commander, leading large groups of high-performing Americans. You don't do that by staying an introvert. You train yourself to grow. You become someone who can stand in front of people and lead. That mindset—if you don't know the answer, find it—has guided me and many others to success.

After leaving the Air Force, I became Director of Safety and Technical Training at Entergy, a Fortune 500 utility company. I was responsible for the safety and training of around 5,000 linemen across four training centers in four states. It's dangerous work. I was asked, "What can I do about it?" a lot, especially after tragedies, like when a young lineman, with kids on the way, lost his life in an accident.

That same question—"What can we do about it?"—led me to run for the United States Senate in 2014. A small group of veterans approached me. They were frustrated that the Republican

Party had backed someone they saw as a former Democrat. They asked me to step up. So I did.

In the military, I faced the same question again and again. *What can I do about it?* Suicide rates among service members were skyrocketing. In 2011, the Army had 362 active-duty suicides—nearly one per day. The Air Force wasn't far behind. I've had mothers who lost sons come to me and ask, "What can you do about it?" I've tried to help them find meaningful ways to serve others, to honor their loved ones.

The same goes for the bigger issues facing America today: waste, fraud, abuse at every institution, public and private, with our tax dollars funding every degeneracy here and abroad you can possibly imagine and even those so dark you can't.

I've stayed involved, especially in the military. I serve on the board of advisors for STARRS—Stand Together Against Racism and Radicalism in the Services. It was founded by Air Force Academy graduates to push back against DEI policies that reminded them of Soviet-style political officers. The Academy even introduced "purple ropes" to identify and report anyone who spoke against Diversity, Equity, and Inclusion (DEI) initiatives, which in practice discriminate on the basis of sex, race, religion, and more. When I learned about STARRS, I stepped in to help spread the word.

I also stay active in fighting government corruption. I lived in Louisiana for eleven years—some would say America's most corrupt state, by many measures. I now live in Mississippi, which also has its share of the same problems.

"What can I do about it?"

Sometimes the answer is a Hollywood action movie, like an adrenaline-soaked mission flown under cover of darkness. Other times, it's closer to home. I have a couple of close family members who are extreme liberals, and that's putting it conservatively. About a year ago, I attended a funeral for another relation. After the service, during the reception (in the South, there's always food afterward), I sat down next to them.

The elder of the two, who's been going blind, said, "Is that Roby?"

I replied, "Yes, it's Roby."

"I've got a bone to pick with you. Why are you supporting this Trump guy? He is a Nazi," she said.

I asked her calmly, "Do you want Social Security to stay viable for your daughters?"

She said yes. "Do you want Medicare to stay viable?"

She said yes. Then I explained how President Trump's policies could strengthen the economy, increase revenues, and reduce inflation—directly helping those programs.

By the end of the reception, she walked over with her cane and said, "Roby, I'm a lot more comfortable with you again now. Thanks for talking with me."

What can you do about it?

You can have a conversation. You can stand up for what's right. You can commit yourself to that which you're told you'll never be able to accomplish. I haven't always gotten it right, but I've always tried to do what's right. I rose to leadership positions most people said weren't possible from where I started. How? Determination. Doing the right thing when the odds were against me. Relying on gut instinct, shaped by family, experience, and values passed down to me.

I found what I can do about "it."

Now, what about you?

CHAPTER 2

It's Your Turn to Do Something Now

"What can I do about it?"

That's the number one question I receive from regular listeners of my show, *The Rob Maness Show*. Over and over again.

But first—what is "it"? And why must we stop it? Well, if you've asked or even wondered about it, you already know what it is. It is a placeholder. For some, it's fighting corruption. For others, it's securing local elections. For many, it's helping ensure Republican victories. Ending resentment-driven DEI programs. Keeping perverts out of girls' sports. Throughout my career, it included all of these in one form or another. But sometimes it took a different form. For me personally, suicide among service members called me to action.

Whatever it is for you, the common thread is this: you see injustice, you feel its impact, and you want it to stop. And more than anything else, the problem is personal.

Maybe you have a little girl who plays soccer. You worry about whether an older, stronger boy—dressed in a wig—might be alone with her in the bathroom. Maybe you have a son. And like me, you're white. Will he be accepted into his top-choice school? Or will his skin color and sex disqualify him from opportunities?

As I write this, there are viral videos on social media of everyday Americans being assaulted simply for wearing a MAGA hat, sporting a Trump-Vance bumper sticker, or even owning a Tesla. Ironically, about 40 percent of Tesla owners are Democrats. They are attacking their own. Property destroyed. People beaten. These radicals are so consumed by hatred they'll even sacrifice their beloved climate cause if it means punishing someone they view as the enemy. The depth of this hatred is breathtaking.

Some of you lost a family member, a close friend, or even a spouse during the draconian COVID-19 policies under the Biden administration. Isolation. Forced vaccines. Job losses. Income destruction. Worse. Many never received justice or even acknowledgment of the devastation they endured.

Or maybe you lost the relationship, not the person, because they became convinced that your patriotism—your love of country, family, and God—was somehow an existential threat to their identity.

Others have suffered the slow destruction of community. The unraveling of high-trust American culture. Policies that, over decades, separated spouses, divided parents from children, and damaged the very fabric of family itself. Maybe you've lost a spouse. Maybe you've seen your child lose their parent. Maybe you've seen it happen to your sibling. Maybe it happened to you.

While we're living it now, none of this is new. We've seen this before. America has lived through periods of low-intensity violence:

- The 1850s conflict over slavery and abolitionism
- The early 1900s battles between unionists and non-unionists

- The Jim Crow violence against the Civil Rights Movement from the 1920s through the 1960s

There's a common root. Unfairness. You and those you love have been mistreated. Unjustly. And at the time, you could do nothing. But the experience left you with a deep, irreversible thought: *This has to stop.*

So what then must start in its place? We cannot just be against things, but know what we are *for*. For me, it's this:

GUNNER WEIGH'S AMERICA

When I was seventeen, I became the youngest person to enter Explosive Ordnance Disposal (EOD) training in the entire United States military, to my knowledge. The first phase was academic— all books and theory. The second was practical. We had to use tools to render ordnance, like IEDs, safe. To survive, you had to become an expert. The attrition rate was 70 percent during Phase Two. Many were NCOs or officers. The median age was thirty-five. I was less than half that. Just a kid. When I got to the first test in the tools phase, I failed. I retested. Failed again.

Our class leaders were two Marines—Sergeant Garcia and Lieutenant Bell. Lieutenant Bell was a Cajun with combat experience in Vietnam. They pulled me aside, this skinny enlisted kid, and introduced me to Marine Warrant Officer "Gunner" Weigh, the instructor for tools. A black man.

Sergeant Garcia said, "We're going to send you to spend the afternoon with him. He'll teach you. And when we pin on those EOD badges, we want you to be there."

Gunner Weigh had been to the jungles of Vietnam three times. This was the late '70s. He spent the entire afternoon with me. Patient. Methodical. He knew I wasn't mechanically inclined—of me and my three brothers, I was the least inclined. But he gave me seven hours of his time, working with me until 8:00 p.m. The next morning, I passed the test. Six months later, I graduated.

Only later did I learn that Gunner Weigh had led EOD teams behind enemy lines. He recovered bodies and classified material at crash sites deep in the jungle—sometimes alone. On his last tour, he was ambushed while recovering a body. His partner was shot in the legs. Couldn't move. Weigh carried him seven miles through the jungle under fire, shot sixteen times himself. The partner was a white Southern kid. Gunner Weigh didn't care. He saw a brother in arms.

And he didn't have to spend that day with me. But because he did, I accomplished everything I did in my career. I exceeded even my own expectations.

This matters. Because those are the kind of Americans we need today. Men like Sergeant Garcia, Lieutenant Bell, and Gunner Weigh. Not the division we see today. Not the suspicion and hate.

Do you want these kinds of men as your neighbors? Or do you want to live divided, isolated, and afraid?

AMERICANS FIRST

- "America First" has returned. But before it was "America First," it was simply *American First*. That's how those men saw me. Not as white Not as Southern. Just as an American.

Some people call it populism. Some call it conservatism or classical liberalism. All of those labels can be helpful. But none of them capture the essence of what we are like Americanism does. We thrive on the values of the Declaration of Independence. We are adamantly supportive of the Founding, especially the Constitution. And we believe in its proper function.

One reason people love President Donald J. Trump is that he isn't wedded to an ideology or to abstract "principles." Personally, I consider myself a libertarian, philosophically. I am friends with Austin Petersen and Senator Rand Paul. But fundamentally, I am an Americanist. We believe in liberty. We believe that the government exists to protect that liberty. And we aren't afraid to use laws or policies, even if they seem contrary to certain economic doctrines, when those laws protect American liberty.

Take tariffs. Free-market purists despise them. Libertarians may recoil. Yet tariffs put America first because they put Americans first. It's Americanist. Populist, conservative, libertarian—they all leave something out, in my view.

An Americanist asks: *Is this good for Americans?* Then makes the decision, without regard to labels.

During his first term, President Trump said[1], "I am a nationalist and proud of it." He loves our country. As do I. We believe in American excellence. In Divine Providence. We know this nation has done more good for more people than any other nation in history. We've had Americanist presidents before. George Washington. Theodore Roosevelt, often called a progressive. Even JFK, a liberal Democrat, was an Americanist at heart.

It's not about abstract principles; it's about purpose. That purpose is simple, for each of us. It is the backdrop, the keystone, the foundation, the peak, whatever your metaphor, it's why we're here right now—I, writing this, and you, reading it. **We're here to do something about it**. About anything that threatens the prosperity of the American people. It starts with you—your family, your home, your business or career, your neighborhood, your community—and it moves outward. Because it must. One light must light the others. Otherwise, we will keep making the

---

1   Fox News, "Trump: I Am a Nationalist and I Am Proud of It," video, October 23, 2018, Fox News video.

very same mistake year after year, election after election. You are probably familiar with it.

Like me, you are sick and tired of watching people vote against their own best interests. I've seen it up close and personal. When I ran for the United States Senate in Louisiana because the Republican Party put up Bill Cassidy—a government doctor, a max donor to Democrat Mary Landrieu, and a former Democrat himself. He was a party man.

I walked into Republican meetings, the only lifelong Republican in my family, and what did I hear? "We're supporting Cassidy. You can't do it. You don't know anything." Some version of that every day on the primary campaign trail.

I had been in the Air Force for over thirty years. I commanded the sixth-largest base in the world, with more nuclear weapons than anyone else. But somehow, I "didn't know anything." So I told them what would happen.

I said, "Cassidy will vote like Mary Landrieu. He won't support you on abortion. He won't put you first." And he didn't. He followed the party line. He fed the military-industrial complex. He even voted to convict President Trump in the second impeachment—a sham if there ever was one. Even today, I still get calls asking me to run against him again.

It's not just Louisiana. You see it in Florida's 6th district. In Pennsylvania. In Wisconsin. Even in Trump's plus-30 districts. People vote against their own interests. For no good reason except, "He's the one we picked."

That's the problem. And that's our challenge. There are still too many people in our own party who refuse to embrace Americanism. As long as that's the case, we'll keep getting inconsistent candidates—and losing winnable races.

This book offers the solution, and not just for elections, but for everything upstream and down; from culture clashes to education policies, to sweeping changes in society, to what happens in your own home under your own authority. Americanism covers all.

Now, there are two parts to doing something about it—whatever the "it" is that you simply cannot tolerate any longer. First, you must become the kind of person who can follow through. Even when you are hated. Even when you are slandered. Even when the threats are real. And second, you need to take decisive, step-by-step action—locally, practically, and persistently.

You must learn to get past the narrative-machine. You must find the actual problems. Even with a Trump win, bureaucracy and legacy media will fight tooth and nail. That said, you don't need to be a genius. You just need to know yourself, what tools you have, and what tools you may still need. And you must ask:

What am I willing to do about it? Am I willing to take the next step? What are the risks? What's my next move? Do I need a team? Family? Friends? Do I have the courage? Physical courage and moral courage?

Decide now. Are you willing? Will you follow through? What you ultimately do about it could be as simple as reading to kids at the library. Volunteering for your township's Citizen Patrol. Or helping get good people elected.

But you must decide. This is the way for Americans who want to serve something greater than themselves.

Why do people keep asking me this question, "What can I do about it?" Because I'm honest. Because if I don't have the answer, I'll go out and find it.

If you're a keyboard warrior, this book is for you. If you want to make a real difference, this book is for you. If you are tired of memes and slogans and ready to take ground, this book is for you.

Right now, we need men—and women—with chests, like President Theodore Roosevelt. And if that's you, let the desire of your heart be Isaiah 6:8.

Then I heard the voice of the Lord saying, "Whom shall I send? And who will go for us?" And I said, "Here am I. Send me!"

Here you are. Let's go.

PART I

What to Do About It (And How to Do It)

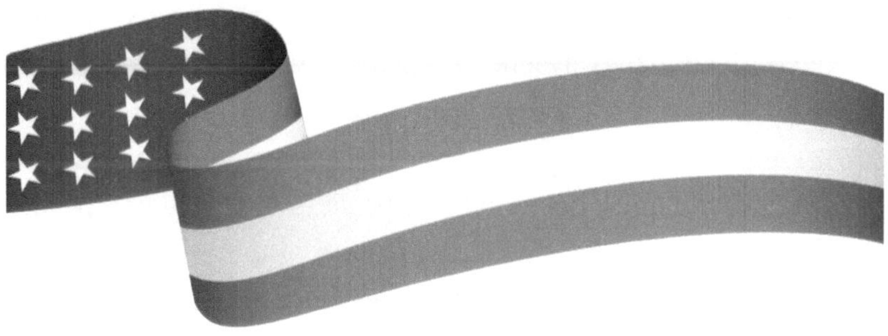

If you're feeling overwhelmed by everything happening around you—the corruption, the chaos, the attacks on our way of life— guess what? **That's how you're supposed to feel.** In these next chapters, you'll learn why feeling overwhelmed isn't a reason to despair; it's a signal. It's the moment to act.

The pain we feel as we see our country slip away—the frustration, the anger, the exhaustion—is the beginning of massive change. Pain is the sign that change is necessary, possible, inevitable even. And Part I shows how to use that pain to fuel decisive action, not endless complaining.

You'll learn how real victories are won: not by scattering your energy, not by fighting every battle at once, but by overwhelming the enemy's efforts with a single, targeted move. You'll see how history's most unlikely victories—from the halls of Washington, DC to culture-war battlefields alive with action—were achieved by individuals who understood how to find the enemy's center of gravity and strike it with overwhelming effect.

You'll also see why the people who succeed at changing the world aren't usually the insiders. They're the ones who still have fresh eyes, who can see the situation clearly because they haven't been corrupted by the system's assumptions. In doing so, I'll also be stripping away some old mental models you may not have even known are holding you back. You will see today's battles for what they really are—and spot opportunities others will miss.

You'll also study a tactic the enemy never expects: embracing and amplifying their own strategies. Instead of reacting to their provocations or running from their narratives, you'll learn how to turn their weapons back on them peacefully, strategically, and decisively. You'll know how to create a situation they cannot escape without collapsing their own authority.

Finally, you'll get lots of examples of great men of American history. You'll glean from them what you need to win back territory here and now—while staying true to who you are.

And that's only Part I. Let's go.

CHAPTER 3

The Pain of Change

After I retired from the military in 2011, I began to network with other veterans also freshly reentering civilian life. This is normal. What's not is who I happened to find myself surrounded by—politically aware and engaged vets, from the Air Force and otherwise. Through a number of providential conversations, I began to realize that both the elected and institutional political leaders in the Republican party (I'd been lifelong GOP at that point) were advertising themselves as pro-Constitution, pro-"peace through strength," and pro-individual rights. They said all the right things; and they did none of it. In reality, they voted, ruled, and otherwise made policy in ways to strip citizens' negative rights, expand blatantly unconstitutional and simply made-up "positive" rights (I'll explain in a moment the difference), and invest more in unjust global wars. In the Middle East, the Arab Spring has sprung months prior. Unnecessary interventionism in otherwise semi-stable countries brought death and doom upon untold numbers of innocents and livelihoods. Then-President Barack Obama led the way; the GOP marched to the beat of his drum. Meanwhile, at home, citizens saw our negative rights slip away (negative meaning the Constitution *forbids* the government from *taking* these rights from you), particularly with regard to freedom of speech, freedom of religion and of association, and of the right to keep and bear arms. Even as President Obama and the Republican-majority US Congress worked in lockstep to extend to Americans *positive* rights (meaning the government *has to* provide something to you, constitutional or not!). Healthcare, housing, and handouts to illegal immigrants (not even citizens!) meant the federal government robbed Peter to pay Paul. Or should I say, Pablo?

Obamacare and *Dreamers* were the two hot topics of that political season. Conservative influencers in both the public and private sectors wrote in bestselling books, gave passionate speeches, and accrued audiences in the millions, who demanded Republicans resist the erosion of freedom in America (this was before mass social media made content distribution and consumption much easier in the late 2010s and 2020s). The people felt that famous quote from the *Network* viscerally, "I'm mad as hell, and I'm not going to take this anymore." Republican officials agreed in spirit. But they talked the mad and acted glad, giving President Obama's radical agenda "bipartisan support" that only ever goes one way.

These are the conversations we had in 2011. The foundational complaint was this: Conservative leaders showed no interest in listening to citizens who weren't part of the accepted DC pundit class or lobbyist crowd, no matter how successful we the people were in real life. And so it was in this environment that a group of fellow veterans recruited me to run for office there in Louisiana in 2013 and 2014 against Bill Cassidy (he's what we call a "RINO," or "Republican In Name Only"). My first supporters (and campaign funders) saw the need to drive our nation back toward a constitutional republic that protects liberty, avoids endless wars, and implements small government policies for our prosperity. We saw the need for massive change in our country—and inside the GOP itself—and set out to do what we could to start that change.

Our issues were simple:

- End the endless war policy.

- Secure the border.

- Achieve energy independence within five years.

What does that remind you of? Perhaps "America First" priorities? Even those that would "Make America Great Again"? Yes; it could be argued that I was "MAGA" before MAGA. Even so, we had no idea how difficult the challenge would be—or even if we could win the Jungle primary against two well-known Louisiana political names. But we quickly realized we were on the right path when millions in small-dollar donations began pouring in.

In my view, this was the continuation of the 2010 TEA Party surge, which was a grassroots movement in 2008 and 2009 in response to President Obama's unprecedented, and frankly unpresidential executive overreach this nation had not witnessed since the days of FDR. *TEA* stood for "Taxed Enough Already." The welfare underclass that carried Obama to the White House wanted handouts, and he was poised to provide them. It was the TEA Party that began the true fight—one that has been very painful ever since—to move our country toward Americanism and away from globalism and the so-called "international rules-based new world order" constructed by the American military-industrial complex after World War II.

Here we are today, more than a decade later, in Donald Trump's second term as President. As of this writing many victories have been won. We have suffered losses. And yet we press on. Because we must. We see the scale of the changes still needed. There is much to do; there is much we can do about it.

Meanwhile, the opposition's determination is also evident. They are willing to use everything—from "lawfare" to the violence of domestic terrorism—to stop us. In the headlines the week I write this, embittered liberals are storming the streets in millions, firebombing, shooting, and otherwise destroying Tesla vehicles and dealerships as revenge against Elon Musk for his support of President Trump during the campaign and afterwards, and otherwise agitating at the local and statehouse level across the country for radical, far-left, frankly *unhuman* policies, like the legalized mutilation and castration of teenagers and children troubled by gender dysphoria. As bad as they are, they show us they can get worse.

THE PAIN OF CHANGE

All of this incenses you, as it does me. It's enraging. It's painful. We think, *I can't stand for this*. This is good. Pain is the beginning of change. As the saying goes, "Nothing changes until the pain of remaining the same is worse than the pain of changing." This is true generally and specifically—and individually. I didn't do something—run the first America First campaign—until I "couldn't take it anymore." I didn't fight for my country's interests only to return home and see my work being undone with great haste and much glee. I couldn't take it anymore. Pain is the beginning of change.

Here's another saying, this one favored by left-wing bad actors: "Silence is violence." Ironically, it's true. If you don't resist it, you support it, whatever the "it" may be. What you allow, you endorse. What you let slide, you let stay. This, by the way, is how families of addicts often react in dysfunction to their loved one with a substance abuse problem—they make a bad situation worse by showing "mercy" or "kindness" to the otherwise unrepentant. The Left wanted to win at all costs; the Right "just wanted to be left alone" to live "socially liberally, fiscally conservative." How'd that work out? Left-wing institutions—education, the media, federal bureaucracies—have been owned and infiltrated by the Left since the 1950s and 1960s. We didn't stop them. We didn't hold them. We didn't counter-infiltrate. And so here we are.

Today, it feels like facing an army of Goliaths. Each of us feels like a David. We look to our King Sauls—our so-called "principled conservative" leaders—and what do we hear? Moaning and groaning about how powerful the enemy is, even as Republicans control the Executive branch, the Legislative branch, the Judicial branch (in theory), and the vast majority of statehouses and governorships across the country.

We don't have to wait on Saul. If you see something, you can say something; if you feel something, you can do something about it. Pain has purpose. Use it. That's how my primary campaign brought America First principles and priorities to the national stage. And I wasn't the only one who was "mad as hell" in 2011.

I'd like you to meet Robbye St. Pierre. When I was first recruited to run for office, I met a lot of people at the grassroots level—leaders in the TEA Party movement locally. One of them passed away, unfortunately, likely from COVID-19 in November 2019. That was Robbye.

Robbye St. Pierre was the daughter of a Texas oil family. She had inherited all of it. If you know anything about Texas oilmen, put that into a woman. Think female Billy Bob Thornton in *Landman*. She pulled an oxygen cart behind her while chain-smoking cigarettes. Her father had a plaque made that she hung over the toilet in her bathroom. It said something to the effect of, "I'll do anything for you, but I'm not going to give you $10,000 to put fake boobs on your chest." That's the kind of family they were. Very wealthy, although you wouldn't know it by talking to Robbye. She was just a regular American citizen. Inspired by the movement.

Besides the local veterans, Robbye was the person who got me thinking about what needed to happen in this country—and what had gone wrong. She lived in New Orleans, but her businesses were all in Texas. She wasn't "government" at all. She didn't take government funding. I don't even think she took Social Security. But she could describe what needed to change better than just about anyone, in simple, direct language. Politicians were being elected based on what they said—and then doing the opposite once they got into office. That made her mad.

As hell.

Robbye wasn't even a lifelong Republican. She started out as a Texas Democrat. That doesn't mean much today, but back then, it did. She eventually walked away completely—not just from the Democrats but from the establishment Republican Party too.

Even though the Republican Party platform still espouses the right Americanist values, the party apparatus still wields too much power. Even today. The establishment still cloaks itself as one thing to get elected—and then shows who they really are. Just like we saw with Bill Cassidy.

Robbye was a country girl with city street smarts; she could spot these types, and she made a lot of noise about them. And she never let up.

I remember her attending TEA Party meetings in Jefferson Parish, Louisiana, as late as 2019—still pulling that oxygen tank, still smoking her cigarette. This was 2019. She said what needed to be said:

- "Your taxes are too high."

- "Your climate regulations are killing my business."

- "We don't need to be taking foreign oil."

- "Get us out of these wars—you're killing our kids for no reason."

- "Secure the border. My competitors are hiring illegals and undercutting me."

Robbye would get red in the face and cuss and just tell people like it was. She was bent on change. Till the day she died. Unlike many Republican officials, she did more than talk.

Did Robbye St. Pierre actually change anything? Absolutely. By supporting candidates like me—Rob Maness—she and people like her, changed the political base of the Republican party in Louisiana. Remember, I wasn't born there. I was a transplant, coming out of the military. My primary opponents' campaign spokespeople even called me a "carpetbagger." But we shook the pillars of the establishment Republican party in Louisiana—the RINO structure collapsed and was never rebuilt.

If you look at Louisiana's government today, they eventually elected Jeff Landry—a TEA Party guy—as governor. I had supported him early on when he ran for Attorney General, after he was drawn out of his congressional seat by establishment Republicans. So yes, people like Robbye St. Pierre and others in that little Jefferson Parish organization changed Louisiana politics. They made a real effort at change in federal politics, too. We came within a six point swing of beating Bill Cassidy in the jungle primary and polled at 53 percent head-to-head against Mary Landrieu. It was close. Very close to having an America First US Senator from Louisiana—before Donald Trump entered politics. And it wasn't because of me. It was because of people like Robbye St. Pierre.

One of the biggest things Robbye did for my campaign was build the statewide volunteer network working with our volunteer State-Wide Volunteer Coordinator Kelly Camp, using TEA Party groups all across the state. It was so effective that when Senator Ted Cruz announced he was running for president in 2016, he called me and asked if he could use my statewide volunteer group. I put him in touch with Robbye. I supported Cruz in the 2016 primary. Back then, he was seen as one of the leaders of the TEA Party movement. Robbye and Kelly built Cruz's statewide volunteer network based on what they had built for me. That wasn't me. That was Robbye and Kelly—and others like the president of that TEA Party group, a woman named Mary Kass.

Mary was just a mom and a wife who worked for a company at the Port of New Orleans. Somehow she found time to lead that Greater New Orleans TEA Party group alongside Robbye. Between them, they did incredible things between 2013 and 2019. Even after Robbye died in 2019, her impact lived on. "Local action has national impact," as General Michael Flynn (ret.) says.

Another issue Robbye, Mary, Sara Wood and others organized against was Common Core in Louisiana, the catastrophically poor educational curricula forced into schools in all fifty states (and into tens of millions of homes to drive parents crazy). These women helped start the statewide coalition that ended Common Core. I helped—but as a talking head for the initiative, a known name.

Think about that: Common Core had millions of dollars behind it. The biggest Republican donors in Louisiana helped to smuggle these left-wing anti-education textbooks and schoolwork into the state in 2010. Bobby Jindal, the Republican governor at the time, supported it—the original "woke" propaganda forced into impressionable young minds! (Though to be fair, he pulled back to a slightly defensible position, directing the state board of education and the state legislature to replace Common Core with "Louisiana standards and a Louisiana test[2]," although it was very similar to the original.

A group of grassroots citizens—with no megadonor funds and no establishment backing—killed it by 2016. They couldn't

____

2   Danielle Dreilinger, "Bobby Jindal's Common Core Announcement," *NOLA.com | The Times-Picayune*, June 18, 2014, http://www.nola.com/education/index.ssf/2014/06/ bobby_jindals_common_core_anno.html.

raise much money because everyone was scared of the Republican leadership at the time. But they didn't quit. TEA Party activists took on their own party, fought the machine, and won. Local action, national impact. A few women, a coalition of mothers, working, stay-at-home, and home-school moms, saw something, and they did something. And it wasn't the politicians who made it happen—it was grassroots citizens like Robbye St. Pierre, Mary Kass, and Sara Wood.

There's another twist to Common Core fight worth mentioning. After Bobby Jindal left office, John Bel Edwards, a Democrat, was elected governor. He's a West Point graduate, head of the Honor Committee at West Point, and a former Guardsman. A solid guy, in my humble opinion. President Donald Trump invited him to White House meetings during the COVID-19 pandemic response because he implemented the president's recommended policies and procedures.

We'll come back to John Bel Edwards in a moment. Now, for a little more context, two of the top three Republican donors in Louisiana—Lane Grigsby and Eddie Rispone, both construction men—wcrc on video, proud to take credit for bringing Common Core to Louisiana. That didn't sit right with me. In 2019, Eddie Rispone ran for governor against John Bel Edwards. In the Republican jungle primary, I had backed Ralph Abraham, a congressman, Army Ranger, and physician—a modern Renaissance man. But Rispone, with his money, beat Abraham in the primary. Rispone's campaign brought President Trump down to Louisiana three times to show his support. That's where it got tough for me. I had supported President Trump since he won the Republican primary in 2016. But I could not, in good conscience, support Eddie Rispone. I even made a video opposing Rispone, wearing a Make America Great Again hat, explaining exactly why I couldn't support him:

- He was one of the men who brought Common Core into Louisiana.

- He testified for it.

- He helped fund it.

I couldn't betray heroines like Robbye St. Pierre, Mary Kass, and Sara Wood, who fought so hard to get rid of Common Core. And as it turned out, Rispone lost; John Bel Edwards was reelected in 2019. And while Edwards wasn't perfect, he was far better than a man who supported policies that hurt our children, in my view.

That decision cost me politically. I had to resign my position on the Republican Executive Committee in our parish. For the first time in my life, I wasn't a Republican anymore—I registered as an independent. Eventually, I moved to Mississippi and rejoined the Republican party. But at that moment in 2019, I knew I had made the right decision.

I couldn't look Robbye St. Pierre's family—or the other grassroots activists who had fought so hard—in the eye if I had supported someone like Rispone, even though it put me at odds with them.

Sometimes, you have to choose between what's politically easy and what's morally right. I learned that from Robbye, as she taught it in her own way. And even after her death, Robbye St. Pierre continued to influence my decisions. That's the kind of woman she was; that's the impact real grassroots leaders have. They live on like legends. Larger-than-life myths. American folk heroes. I will never forget Robbye St. Pierre. And now, neither will you.

Everything I had learned in my life up to that point, and people I met like Robbye, gave me the clarity to make the right choice—even when it was hard. Others I know personally fit the same mold—people who felt the pain, couldn't take it, and said in word or deed . . . **no**.

People like Kelly Camp. She was volunteer coordinator during my first campaign and my field director during my second

US Senate campaign and later for a statehouse race. She's now a close family friend. A key attribute for this story is that she is a cradle Catholic who had fallen away from her faith and through our work together re-discovered that faith and is now a devout practicing Catholic. As you might have guessed, Kelly is one of the fiercest pro-life activists I've ever met.

She helped mentor me on life-from-conception, politically. Coming of age in the Air Force and serving there most of my life, I didn't focus on politics. I voted for whoever I thought would be best for the country. I didn't understand sociopolitical trench warfare—like the right-to-life movement. Kelly opened my eyes.

I've seen her stand up in Republican women's meetings and call out politicians for defending pro-choice policies—right to their faces—which from the Catholic perspective are better termed *pro-death*. That's fair. Because that's what they are. Some issues are gray. Others are black and white. The right to life is one of them.

John Kennedy, now a US Senator from Louisiana, used to be a Democrat. Back when he was exploring running for Senate, he didn't have a strong pro-life stance. Kelly and others like her were relentless in their pressure, in their persuasion. They stood up, said what they believed, and demanded answers. Thanks to everyday women like Kelly, the grassroots activists with deep moral conviction, Louisiana eventually passed strong pro-life laws—even with a Democrat governor. In fact, a black Democrat woman in Louisiana brought the original bill to set a fifteen-week limit on abortion. From WBUR.org:

> *[Governor Edwards supports] the so-called "heartbeat" bill, which makes the procedure illegal once a heartbeat is detected. He is the U.S.'s only anti-abortion Democratic governor.*
>
> *A number of Democrats backed the bill in the state legislature, one of them being Rep. Katrina Jackson . . . who is African American.*

"African American babies are being aborted at alarming numbers," she tells Here & Now's Robin Young. In an interview with NBC News, Jackson said she considers abortion to be "modern-day genocide."

She says she supports the state's move to outlaw abortion after a fetal heartbeat is detected—with no exception for rape or incest—because abortion shouldn't be "touted as the answer for African Americans who live in poverty situations."

The heartbeat bill was signed into law by Governor John Bel Edwards. That didn't happen by accident. It happened because people like Kelly Camp and the grassroots wouldn't let up. And after *Roe v. Wade* was overturned, Louisiana went even further— banning almost all abortions except in cases of a life-threatening emergency to the mother[3].

I've attended candlelight protests with Kelly Camp and Mary Kass—and priests, nuns, and Catholic laypeople—outside of proposed Planned Parenthood clinics throughout Louisiana. Where do they try to build these clinics? In black neighborhoods, as Representative Jackson understands. Just like McDonald's puts stores based on demographics, Planned Parenthood places clinics where they believe they'll have "customers." It's, in a word, evil. We protested night after night at one site in New Orleans, and they eventually dropped the project.

This is the lesson: You don't have to sit down and take it. You can stand up. You can say no. Even if you're just one person in a crowd, you make a difference.

In those protests, I wasn't a leader. I was just a citizen who cared about protecting babies. As Americans, we believe in the right to life, liberty, and the pursuit of happiness. That starts at conception. A baby in the womb is an American citizen. And as

---

3   Louisiana State Legislature, "La. Rev. Stat. § 14:87.1," *Louisiana Laws*, accessed April 21, 2026, https://legis.la.gov/legis/Law.aspx?d=97020.

Christians, we're commanded to protect those who cannot defend themselves. That's why I'm 100 percent pro-life. The end of *Roe v. Wade* is just the beginning.

Yes, politically, sometimes you have to message around exceptions like rape or incest because that's what wins elections. President Trump understands that. But personally, I don't believe in exceptions. Life is life. Always. Most OB-GYNs will tell you that cases where the mother's life is at risk are incredibly rare. And by the third trimester, you can deliver the baby and save both lives.

Effective grassroots warriors brings me to another important point: veterans. Most of the veterans I know—especially those active in grassroots politics—are publicly (and loudly) against endless wars. It's the ones who've actually been in the fight who understand. In my own Republican Party Executive Committee here in Harrison County, Mississippi—the biggest Republican county in the state—the chairman is a veteran. The vice chairman is a veteran. The treasurer is a veteran. And they are adamantly against the endless war policies that have defined recent decades. They believe in peace through strength. We lived through the Cold War. We saw President Reagan's deterrent strategy work. The Soviet Union collapsed without a shot being fired because we projected strength.

Now consider Ukraine. Most of the veterans I know look at what's happening and say, *This is crazy*. I know veterans who don't even agree with taking direct action against the Houthis in the Red Sea, even though they've attacked US Navy vessels over 300 times. Peace through strength works. But weakness welcomes war. That's where we've been as a global power.

When it comes to Ukraine, most people don't know the full story. I've been tracking Ukraine since about 2008, even before I left the Air Force. The US and British governments have taken actions inside Ukraine that led directly to what's happening today. There were two color revolutions—the first around 2008, another in 2014 that pushed out the neutral (not "pro-Russian") leader. It pains me to say this as someone who served during the Cold War, but what's happened in Ukraine is a direct consequence of Western meddling. That doesn't mean I'm "pro-Putin." He's a KGB colonel, after all; once a Soviet, always a Soviet. It's just fact: Russia's invasion wasn't "unprovoked." Ethnic Russians in Eastern Ukraine were being attacked. There were real atrocities committed by groups like the Azov Battalion—Ukrainian nationalists with Nazi heritage stretching back to World War II. That history matters. Propaganda won't change the facts.

I'm no fan of Vladimir Putin. He's a dictator. He rigs elections. He's consolidated power in himself. But there's a critical difference between modern Russia and the Soviet Union: Russia today protects Christianity. That's significant. And it's why I don't believe Russia will ever return to Soviet-style communism. Still, we cannot have 20th century-style wars anymore. Humanity can't survive another one.

One of the main reasons I agreed to run for office the first time was because of the endless war policy. In fact, that was my number-one issue in my first campaign. I was in the Pentagon on 9/11. I supported the initial response to that attack. That was a just war. But by 2005, it wasn't a just war anymore. When I left my last combat tour in 2005, we briefed our two-star general boss the following:

- We have no strategy.

- Our only task is to send planes into kill boxes and wait for calls for close air support.

- We have achieved victory by removing the Taliban and al-Qaeda from Afghanistan.

- It's time to go home.

- Why? We've accomplished the mission. We can hand Afghanistan back to its people.

But we didn't. We stayed. And we turned a just war into an endless, unjust catastrophe. Every year we stayed after that created more enemies for America—and got more Americans killed unnecessarily. And it continues. Even as I write this, we still have boots on the ground in the Middle East, making our young men and women targets without a vital national interest at stake. It's inhumane—for them and for the people in those countries. It's also dangerous for America's standing in the world. Weakness invites war.

At the grassroots level today, the veterans I know—especially the ones active in politics—are the most adamant about stopping endless wars. That's why President Trump resonates so much with veterans. He understood that strength deters war, but weakness invites it. Trump isn't a warmonger; he didn't start new wars in his first term. He focused on protecting American lives and interests without unnecessary foreign entanglements.

Now, not everyone agrees. Some veterans, especially older cold warriors, still believe in the old endless war policies that result in disasters like Afghanistan and missteps like we're making in Ukraine. They're the exception, though, and I can understand so. Most of the veterans I know—and the Republican grassroots in places like Mississippi—are sick of endless wars. We want peace. Real peace, built through undeniable American strength.

Local action, national impact. It's the veterans, the moms, the dads, the everyday Americans who show up, organize, run for office, stand up at school boards, refuse to be silent—and change history. We've done it before. We can do it again. You can join us.

There's a lot you probably resonate with in this chapter. Likely, you agree with it all, or the vast majority. You just want to **do** something about it. All of it. Well, any of it. Very good. But like me, you don't have unlimited time. Most of us sure don't have unlimited money. How do we prioritize? What do we "do about it" first? Let's find that out for you next.

What You Can Do About It

CHAPTER 4

Overwhelm the Overwhelm

Let me take you back to the most overwhelming day I ever had in my military career—and that was 9/11. That morning, before the first tower was hit, I'll describe to you exactly what I was doing.

When I went to work that morning, I was serving as a military officer in nuclear operations on the Joint Staff. I had been there a little over a year at that point. Keep in mind, the Nuclear Operations Division on the Joint Staff was essentially the keeper of the key for global nuclear warfare. There were maybe seven or eight of us in total. Among them were civilians—people who were the institutional memory, the core intelligentsia for how the United States fights its biggest and most existential war.

At the time, I worked in a section called Theater Nuclear Operations. I reported directly to a colonel. And here's something I've probably mentioned before: in 2001, the United States did not have a theater nuclear war plan. Only a global one. It was called the Single Integrated Operational Plan, or SIOP, and it covered global nuclear warfare. That's it.

So there we were—two of us, sitting in a corner of the Pentagon, metaphorically speaking, being treated like the guys who play with crayons or pick our noses all day. But we knew better. We convinced leadership that theater commanders—like the Pacific Command (then known as PACOM)—needed actual, real-world theater-level nuclear planning. Because their operational war plans didn't include nuclear weapons integration. At all.

In those days, nuclear warfare was either "global" or it was off the table. Just before 9/11, we had completed our work. We had finalized the decision tools for the first-ever theater nuclear war plan, inserted them into the so-called "black book," and trained the president, military aides, and relevant commanders on how to use it.

So when I walked into work on the morning of 9/11, the U.S. was confident—comfortable in its role as the lone superpower. We believed the only kind of major war we might fight would be nuclear, and that even that was increasingly unlikely. That's not to say we were letting our guard down—we still had our plans, our weapons, and our people. But the prevailing mindset was: global nuclear war isn't coming. We're good.

But by 9:30 a.m., everything changed. Both World Trade Center towers had been hit. The Pentagon had been hit. And we were getting unconfirmed reports of another airplane inbound— possibly heading toward the Capitol. That turned out to be the plane that went down in Pennsylvania. And in that moment, I realized we were completely overwhelmed.

One of the top civilians in charge of the global nuclear war plan—the guy who knew every page and detail—looked at me when I said, "We have just undergone what looks like a strategic attack on the United States. They just hit the world's most powerful military headquarters."

He replied, "Oh, absolutely not. This is some kind of criminal activity."

I stared at him. I said, "I don't know about you, man, but this feels like a strategic-level attack."

We hadn't even evacuated yet. Most of the building had, but we were in the military command center—a more secure part of the Pentagon—so we stayed. And in that moment, I knew: even the best-prepared minds in America—the ones supposed to understand global conflict—were mentally unprepared for what just happened.

We had no idea who did it. No clue. But I could see it for what it was. Commercial aircraft had just been turned into cruise missiles. And in our nuclear war plans, we used cruise missiles to conduct strategic attacks. That was the model.

So when I say we were overwhelmed, I mean it. Completely. For a couple of hours, we were trying to orient ourselves—trying to make sense of the battlefield. Then, once our heads were back on straight, we got to work. Everything I observed, I wrote down as soon as possible afterwards so we could keep ourselves oriented moving forward (a report which you can find in the Appendix, by the way).

In a situation as dark as that, when you're facing overwhelming shock, how do you respond? What do you do to "overwhelm the overwhelm"?

THE ONE THING

At first, you're in reactive mode. Your brain goes into, *How do I respond? How do I react?* And in that mode, the initial decision by leadership was to evacuate the building—a standard peacetime fire evacuation. But that created a new problem. There were about 22,000 people in the Pentagon at that time of day. And that evacuation funneled around 4,000 to 5,000 people out into five open points around the building. Broad daylight. No tree cover. No real protection. And as they worked through the problem set, someone realized: *We've just put thousands of people into five unprotected, concentrated targets.*

Around that same time, we got confirmed reports that Flight 93 was inbound toward the Capitol region. The decision was made to launch F-16 fighters from the DC National Guard base over at Andrews. Their orders were to intercept that aircraft—take it down if necessary.

But then came the decision that shifted everything—one that, in my view, "overwhelmed the overwhelm." All the generals were gathered in the military command center. At the table was the vice chairman of the Joint Chiefs. He was an Air Force general—General Richard Myers, I believe—and he'd just been nominated to be the next Chairman of the Joint Chiefs. Coincidentally, he had just left his role as the commander of NORAD—North American Aerospace Defense Command. He understood the air domain better than anyone in the room. NORAD constantly runs drills—air defense, intercepts, air sovereignty missions. It's routine for them to launch fighters to intercept potential intrusions into U.S. or Canadian airspace. But at that moment in 2001, the U.S. had taken most of its fighters off alert. We were at a historically low state of readiness.

Now, the reason those fighters at Andrews could be launched is that they had been involved in a training exercise that morning. That was a major factor. At the same time, on our end, we had been running our global nuclear warfare exercise. That's why most of the Joint Staff's nuclear operations personnel were deployed to command and control nodes around the world. I was one of the few left in the building.

In fact, the "doomsday" airplane was taking off from Andrews right as the 757 hit the Pentagon. The fighters at Andrews had what's called target practice ammunition. Not ideal. But even that was enough to bring down a commercial airliner if needed. And they would've been launched regardless—even if the only option was to ram the target.

Here's the pivotal moment. General Myers looked across the room at the Secretary of Transportation and said, clearly and directly, **"Land all the airliners. Force them to land. Now."**

That was it. That was the decision that cut through the chaos. It halted the momentum of the attacks. If there was another wave coming—and we thought there might be—that one order disrupted it. Every single commercial aircraft in North America—U.S. and Canada—was ordered to land immediately. Within minutes. If you've never seen the photos of that day, go look them up. You'll see airliners tail-to-tail, covering tarmacs at places like Toronto, Ontario… jammed into airports in ways we've never seen before or since.

That single order—land them all—was elegant, simple, outside-the-box. But it changed everything. It broke the pattern of fear and response. It was the one thing that overcame being overwhelmed. And it came from a single individual, thinking clearly in a crisis.

FINDING YOURS

Now, today, we're living through something that feels similar. Not kinetic war, but a form of psychological and institutional warfare. Think DEI, or the transgender ideology. It's all in our schools. In our libraries. In our universities. Even in the Pentagon. Even still. That ideology took decades to embed. It's written into policies, operating procedures, personnel, and protocols. It's deeply rooted in every level. Donald Trump won the 2024 presidential election, but the war for America is not over. Not even close.

Zoom out from that victory, and we realize the anti-

Americanists have gone nowhere; they've regrouped. And they seek revenge. Even now, this enemy is attacking from every direction—every system, every line of defense we have. If we cannot unite on one decision, we can't respond effectively. So the question is: *What's our one thing?* What's our equivalent of land-all-the-airliners? Not to "win the war" outright—but to break the paralysis. To interrupt the enemy's momentum. To give our side time to regroup, reorient, and respond. What could that be for each of us? What will **your** own decision be that changes everything?

Because just like that day in the Pentagon, it may come down to a single individual making a clear decision (in this case, *you*). No one else in the room on 9/11 had thought of that order. No committee drafted it. No task force approved it. It came from one man. One order. And it made all the difference.

You see, the Secretary of Transportation was the one who had the authority to do it—since he's responsible for the safety of passengers and civilian aircraft. The general didn't have the power to make that order himself.

The reason I bring that up is because that general is like a parent or grandparent watching what's going on in our public schools right now. The indoctrination is everywhere. Grandpa is partially responsible, but he doesn't hold the authority. And he's looking at something that's overwhelming him, just like a parent is looking around going, *Wow, they've even got the kindergartens. They've got the preschools. The universities. The media. The federal government. Local government. It's everywhere.*

And the question becomes: *What do we do? What's that one thing that can actually make a difference? The one thing that has an outsized effect. That the average person—parent, citizen, whoever—can suggest or influence or take part in. What's that?*

Well, let's think it through, using this chapter's opening story as the template: **What was the actual impact of grounding all those airliners?**

It eliminated the threat—or, at least, the unknown threat we believed was still out there. If you've ever looked at a live flight radar map, you'll know what I mean. Just over the U.S. and Canada alone, there are thousands of aircraft in the sky at any given time. If you're trying to find one or two hostile planes in all of that, how do you do it? You land all the aircraft. It's the only way to isolate the threat. Because we knew at that point the terrorists weren't listening to air traffic controllers. We'd already seen that with the hijacked planes. So asking or instructing wasn't going to work. You needed decisive, outside-the-box thinking.

And that reminds me of something I've seen online—a kind of modern-day, individualized version of this idea. There's an anonymous account on X (formerly Twitter) called "DEI for White Guys." What this individual does is write up scripts we can use in corporate settings—in DEI-saturated workplaces or colleges, specifically. It's made for employees who want to start their own "employee resource group" (ERG) for, say, European Americans. Or for a group that promotes "Family Pride," as an alternative to company-sponsored Gay Pride Month festivities.

Now, the point is not that these groups get approved—because they rarely do. The point is to force HR and DEI departments into a corner: If they deny a European-American group, or a men's group, or a Family Pride group, they're now open to a racial or sex discrimination claim. And what's been happening, according to the account, is that HR departments—rather than deal with the legal risk—are shutting everything down. Canceling all the ERGs. Ending the DEI programs across the board. So in a way, it's that one thing that breaks the system—like landing all the airplanes.

It's individual-level. That's the beauty of it. It doesn't require a title or office. You don't have to be in charge of anything. Just a strategic initiative. Similarly, consider what Libs of TikTok founder, Chaya Raichik, did. She got angry about how radical, violent, and cruel left-wing influencers had become—especially around gender ideology pushed onto innocent children.

What's her one thing? She started posting the radical Left's own words and videos. She showed mainstream America exactly what these activists were saying and doing in classrooms, hospitals, libraries. That one move completely disrupted their ability to hide behind euphemisms.

It's the same concept: *Play their game against them. Remove their anonymity. Deprive them of their place on the propaganda board.* And it **works**. Both examples—DEI for White Guys and Libs of TikTok—deal with the world as it is, not as we wish it were.

This is key.

When General Myers told the Secretary of Transportation to land every airliner, he wasn't operating in a fantasy. He wasn't saying, "Well, maybe this will pass," or, "Let's gather more intel first," or, "Let's form a task force." He had a real-world view of the situation—an understanding of where we were, what our vulnerabilities were, and how to stop the bleeding. He didn't act based on what should be true. He acted based on what was true.

In Chapter 5, we're going to talk about the wisdom of heeding fresh eyes. Now, you don't have to be a young person, just new to the scene. General Myers had just stepped into that leadership room. He had a new perspective, which allowed him to see clearly what had to be done.

Chaya and DEI-for-white-guys do likewise; they see the enemy's strategy and tactics as they actually are and how they're impacting the real world. Both of them came up with one idea—just one—that had the same kind of effect as that general on 9/11. They weren't trapped by the same worldview that everyone else around them was stuck in. They saw the battlefield for what it is.

EMBRACE AND AMPLIFY TO WIN WITHOUT A FIGHT

To help you overwhelm the overwhelm—or rather, overwhelm the *overwhelmed* doing that overwhelm—let's describe these two individuals' strategy as the persuasion principle of **"embrace and amplify."** This is where you accept or adopt your opponent's position—and then either take it to the logical extreme. Or, just repeat and spread it more widely than they intended.

Think about it . . . the enemy is using civilian airliners as weapons. So what did General Myers do? He treated every airliner like it was potentially a weapon—and grounded them all. That's embrace and amplify.

Or take Chaya. The radical Left wants an audience for its extremist gender and sexual ideology. Fine. She gives them the audience they said they wanted—by posting their videos to a wider and more mainstream audience. *That's the marketplace of ideas, right? Let's let people see it.*

Same thing with White Guy DEI. He embraces the entire structure: ERGs, diversity, perks, racial affinity groups. Then he applies for an ERG for European-Americans. For straight people. When HR says no, that's racial discrimination—and *boom*, the whole DEI structure collapses. They shut it all down. He didn't oppose the system; he amplified it.

So, where is the enemy strongest? Go there, accept it for what it is—and run with it. Turn their strength into a trap.

Take the city council example we're seeing all over the country. They keep giving special attention to Islamic holidays and holding religious observances in council chambers—but not for any other religion. So what do you do? You accept the premise. "Great! Let's host a Catholic Mass here next month. Or a Jewish prayer service. Or a Christian Bible study." And the second that happens? People freak out. Suddenly, it's all, "Separation of church and state!" And now they have to either allow all religious services—or none. And more often than not, they'll shut it all down. Now the Islamic favoritism ends, too.

Embrace and amplify—take the precedent they created and follow it to its logical conclusion. The same approach could work with school boards. Or local libraries. Or city-funded programs. Take the real world as it is, not as you wish it were—and play the long game from inside their own rules.

There's influence and decision-making at the local level regarding which books get brought in—and which ones get highlighted. And I've seen it even in conservative areas. Libraries that are in 80 percent red counties will still display all the extremist DEI stuff. Anti-white, anti-straight books. You walk into the children's section and the first thing you see is *My Pronouns Are She/Her*, a picture book for preschoolers.

So, the question is: **Who's deciding which books go on display?** You need to be one of the people who decides that. You could either suggest alternatives that are commercially viable— like, "Hey, this is one of the bestselling books in the country right now. Let's display this one instead."

Because then you have an argument that's not ideological— it's practical. "Why are we putting out a book nobody's buying just because it's LGBTQ-themed, when people actually want this other book?" Or, "Why don't we showcase some local authors? Let's host a local event."

And through that, you're indirectly de-platforming all the anti-American, left-wing, cultural Marxist content. Not by fighting it, but by replacing it with something else—something more appealing, more universal, or just more interesting. It's peaceful. It's persuasive.

Or, you go the other direction. You intentionally go hard in the other direction. "You know what? Let's put out the most radical LGBT books—the ones with graphic material—and let parents know we're doing it, in the name of diversity." You intentionally push it so far that the whole program blows up on its own. That's the Libs of TikTok strategy; you amplify the crazy so people can actually see it—and reject it.

Either way, you're doing the thing they don't expect. What does the Left expect from the Right? Outrage. Reaction. Complaints. Podcasts about how mad we are. What they don't expect is to be taken seriously—and to have their logic turned back on them. "Oh, you have an employee resource group for every gender, religion, and ethnicity? Great! Let's start one for Orthodox Christians. Oh, you're not going to allow that? That's discrimination. See you in court."

Then what happens? They shut it all down to avoid the lawsuit. So it's not resistance; it's judo. It's the art of war.

Speaking of which, the day I wrote this chapter was the eighty-third anniversary of the Doolittle Raid. B-25s, twin-engine medium bombers. They were loaded onto the USS Hornet—an aircraft carrier—and launched against Japan. The Japanese believed they were untouchable, that their mainland could never be attacked from the air. No bombers had the range.

Jimmy Doolittle led the mission to change that. I served in the modern-day version of his squadron, the 34th Bomb Squadron—the T-Birds. Doolittle's crew was from that squadron. I met and spent a full day with his navigator, Henry "Hank" Potter, who was in his twenties during the war.

Leading up to the raid, the Pearl Harbor attack by the Japanese empire had just crippled most of our Pacific fleet—except for the carriers. The Japanese thought they had total dominance and time to regroup. They were confident. Arrogant, even.

Then America did the unexpected. We said, in effect, "Let's bomb the Japanese mainland." How? We didn't have planes with that range. Our bombers couldn't land again on the carrier—they had to ditch or crash-land afterward. But we did it anyway. We thought like Chaya. Like that DEI White Guy. Like General Myers on 9/11.

What's the one thing we can do right now that nobody expects, that changes the entire game?

That's what the Doolittle Raid was. Nobody thought it was possible. The navigator I talked to? He had no electronics. Just a compass, a pencil, and an altimeter. And he got them to Tokyo.

That's the kind of thinking we need now. We have to be innovative. Do something they're not expecting. That's classic warfare, and it's how to win. It works on the ground, it works in the air, it works at sea.

Whatever you do, here's what you do: *Take the fight to the enemy.*

And the point of this is, **you don't have to wait**. You don't have to wait for it to get worse. And you definitely don't need to waste all your energy just getting outraged and spreading outrage.

I can liken that to how, in the military, when you're attacking a target set, you don't just go after everything at once. We teach systems analysis. You find the center of gravity in the system—the one critical target that, if you hit it, the rest collapses. That's exactly what Chaya's doing. That's what General Myers did on 9/11. Instead of trying to hit everything, they identified the one thing that really mattered—and neutralized it.

The instinct in a crisis like 9/11 is, "We've got to shoot all the planes down!" because people are dying, and you're panicked. But the smarter approach is to ask, *What's the enemy's center of gravity here?* And in that case, it was that they were using commercial airliners as weapons. So when Myers had all the planes grounded, he cut off the one method of attack.

You don't exhaust yourself reacting to every little thing. You go after the one thing that breaks their entire strategy. And in other contexts, you might not be attacking from the outside—you might infiltrate from the inside. Just like Chaya did. She didn't make reaction videos or post rants. She didn't even show her face. She just reposted their own content. Even the name—Libs of TikTok—sounded like a fan page at first! Nobody even knew who she was for the longest time.

That's similar to the Chinese concept of unrestricted warfare, where you don't win through conventional conflict. You win by infiltrating, by subverting. And the Chinese have been doing it to the West for decades. One example? Convincing our elites to let Confucius Institutes into major U.S. universities.

It's textbook infiltration. I experienced it firsthand. I was selected to attend the Harvard Kennedy School while still in the Air Force. They gave me a year off with pay to go do it. In my class were all kinds of people—adversarial nations and communists. I remember a woman from China, a member of parliament from Tanzania, a man named Ferdinand. He was ex-Soviet Army, it turns out. And then Jerry Adams came through too, from the IRA. He ultimately became Sinn Féin, their political wing. Harvard hosted him; America's most prestigious university hosted our enemies.

That was also the first time and place I ever heard terms like "white privilege" and "critical race theory"— and it came from a black communist activist from New Orleans who was in my class. It blew my mind. But now, looking back, I realize exactly what I was seeing: **infiltration**. Back then, I didn't have the framework to interpret it. I just didn't know what I was looking at.

But looking back from this end of history, you can see the pattern. And Ferdinand? We got suspicious of him. My roommate and I, another B-1 aviator who had flown with me in SAC, were sharing a boarding house. We noticed Ferdinand was a little too sharp. Turns out, he had gone to the Soviet Union's War College. One night, we're at his place for a party, and there's a framed black-and-white class photo on the end table—his War College class. And who's he standing next to? Leonid Brezhnev, the Soviet leader. Right next to him.

So we started our own little informal intelligence op on the guy. For example, we took him to an air show where they had a B-1 on display. At that point, they had removed its nuclear capability. But we wanted to see what kind of questions he'd ask. Just get a read on him. But we took him up into the cockpit—because we knew the crew—and we actually put him in the front seat. We started walking him through how the nuclear bombs and missiles used to be launched from that aircraft. His eyes got big, real big. He was soaking in every word. I'm sure he gave his Soviet handlers a fantastic report afterward. Then he walked us through a display of old Soviet anti-aircraft guns—like museum pieces—and started explaining how his military was still using them. He lit up like a tour guide in Red Square.

That's how they do it. They infiltrate, and they've been doing it for decades. What's so disconcerting is this: What are the most powerful and prestigious institutions in America? Harvard. Wall Street. The Pentagon. The media. The churches. The schools. So they ask, "Where is the influence?" and then they go after it with the most anti-American people and ideas imaginable—and we, the pro-America side, let them. That's been the strategy for thirty-plus years.

Which brings us to the point. If you're reading this right now and something absolutely pisses you off—something in your school district, your city council, your workplace—figure out: *Who's doing it, and where is their power center?* Then, get involved. Volunteer. Join the board. Take the open seat. Start the petition. Push the policy. Run the meeting. Start the campaign.

You don't need anyone's permission. You're in charge now. They're not going to stop you.

Only you will be able to do that. You see, passion can get you started, but it won't keep you going. You need to know more than what you don't want; you need to be able to communicate crisply and clearly what you *do* want. Let's do that next.

CHAPTER 5
Casting Your Vision of Victory

When I was selected to be a Wing Commander in the Air Force, it was the honor of a lifetime, but it was more than honor—it was a challenge. I would be replacing a commander who had failed two nuclear surety inspections. In the years leading up to these failures, America's Air Force had unknowingly flown several nuclear weapons across the entire country, investigated that near catastrophe, and created a new organization to address the issues named Global Strike Command. I was one of the first full colonels to lead the new command as its deputy director of programming and requirements.

The full story is horrifying. Here's what happened: In North Dakota, six cruise missiles with live nuclear warheads were loaded onto a B-52[4]. They were flown in the middle of the night, all the way to Shreveport—Bossier City, Louisiana, specifically—where

---

4   Stephen Losey, "You Can Call 2007 Nuke Mishandling an Embarrassment, but Don't
     Call It the 'Minot Incident,'" *Air Force Times*, June 25, 2019, https://www.airforcetimes.
     com/news/your-air-force/2019/06/25/you-can-call-2007-nuke-mishandling-an-
     embarrassment-but-dont-call-it-the-minot-incident/.

Barksdale Air Force Base is located. The plane landed and was parked on a ramp that wasn't given the level of security normally required for nuclear weapons. Nobody knew. Not the officers on the aircrew. Not the security personnel. Not the maintenance personnel. It was discovered by one of the young airmen—a crew chief. For reference, crew chiefs are the guys and gals who take care of the airplanes themselves. They get them ready to launch, and when the planes come back, rope maintenance experts are needed. And it was the crew chief who found them. You see, there's a little port on the side of the cruise missile where you can look inside. If you see the right indicator inside that port, it tells you: *This is a real warhead.*

The reason I was hired into the command and eventually for the wing commander job is I had built a reputation that I was effective at developing and implementing cultural change in military organizations. I learned early in my career, from combat veterans, that the American war-fighting culture was to be protected and cultivated because it is the core reason why we exist and why we can win when called upon. The culture in nuclear units adds an additional trait that heightens that culture to one, not of zero-defects, but one of war fighting where operational risk management is so effective, an accidental or unintended nuclear detonation will never occur, as near zero as humanly possible. The wing I took command of had obviously lost that culture. Cultural change is the one thing that we can change in societies, organizations, and institutions that drives corrections or progress toward our intended targets. Here's how I did it.

FROM HANDS OFF TO HIGH ACCOUNTABILITY: FINDING THE ONE THING THAT CHANGES EVERYTHING

The very **first** culture change act was to communicate what was to come. Remember, the intent was to revert the culture back to what it once was—when it was effective.

So the first thing I did was bring that up in my speech. Whenever there is a change of command ceremony, the incoming commander gives a speech to set his priorities. Now, in my speech, I didn't say we were going to revert back to a culture. I simply laid out what the culture was going to be—from a nuclear weapons mission perspective.

Of course, I used what I knew. I grew up in Strategic Air Command as a lieutenant. I was well-versed. I had been a nuclear staff officer on the Joint Staff. I had even written pages for the "nuclear football"—the one the president carries with him. I co-wrote war plans that had never existed before. That's why I had been asked to be the first Deputy Director of Programming and Requirements at Global Strike Command—because I was one of the few people left in the Air Force who still understood the culture of the bonded ship. I was one of the first O-6 level colonels assigned there, between 2009 and 2010. I was responsible for building the culture in the new command—specifically in my area, which was programming the budget (PPBS is what they call it at the Pentagon—Planning, Programming, and Budgeting System). I pulled all the assets in, built the budget, formed a team, and laid out future requirements. The B-21 Raider you see today? The team I was on laid down those initial requirements.

Now imagine—after that nuclear weapons incident—how serious the situation was. In the old Strategic Air Command, that never would have happened. Because there was a foundational level of discipline and attention to detail that was legendary—all the way down to the lowest-ranking airman, to each and every seventeen- and eighteen-year-old. It didn't matter whether you were pulling guard duty or crewing an aircraft. That level of attention to detail and discipline was ingrained in everyone because we could not afford an accident—or an unintended detonation of a nuclear weapon. And that level of discipline even extended into how the weapons themselves were designed. We build three or four fail-safes into each nuclear weapon. So three or four different things have to happen—by accident or by intention—in order to get an unintended nuclear explosion. The old-school culture made such a sequence of events virtually impossible.

Here's a hint about that culture. If you ever get a chance, go back and watch Jimmy Stewart's movie *Strategic Air Command*, you'll get a sense of the old Strategic Air Command culture that General Curtis LeMay during World War II started. It's a culture that doesn't insist on zero defects but insists on such discipline, such risk management, and such deep knowledge of your job that you're able to mitigate the risk of an unintended nuclear weapon explosion—whether through accident or, God forbid, theft or malice.

That was the culture. And that's what we were going to recreate. Of course, all the troops were there at the change of command ceremony to hear the speech laying all this out. More importantly, every commander was there. I had four colonels— senior commanders working for me—and about twenty of their subordinate squadron commanders. Then it went down to lower-level unit leaders from there. All the leaders were there. All. And to them all, I laid out the following priority: **disciplined attention to detail**. This single sentence, ultimately fulfilled, would foster a risk mitigation environment. From the President's decision-making process all the way down to the lowest-ranking airman counting rivets on the flight line, that foundation of disciplined attention to detail would be the key to success, to transforming our culture. And that culture would be covering three areas:

- The training environment

- The leadership environment

- The asset environment (meaning the weapons themselves)

Let's talk about what happened that evening, after the command change and the speech. Normally, after a big change of command day for a unit like that, you'd have a day of celebration. After all, the base I was taking command of covered 53,000 acres. About 23,000 people lived and worked there—men, women, and children. Usually, the new commander doesn't really go to work right away. It's a ceremonial day.

- But not for me. I wanted to get going—beyond just my speech. So I called all of my commanders and senior enlisted personnel into the command post, a secure area. I had a briefing ready to go, one I had adapted from an old mentor of mine—a three-star general I worked for as a second lieutenant. He had been the Eighth Air Force commander, and under Strategic Air Command, an even bigger deal. The Eighth Air Force handled the B-52 bombers, B-1 bombers (which were nuclear-capable at one time), and the B-2 bombers. He took what the Eighth Air Force did in Europe during World War II and made it even larger under Strategic Air Command. He was a mentor to me, and I had seen many of his briefings. So, I *stole* his briefing—and made it my own! And so, that evening, I brought in my commanders and laid out what this looks like—what it means to be a disciplined-in-the-details nuclear weapons unit. I had to educate senior leaders on what it means to handle nuclear weapons—what those weapons mean for the United States, for our power in the world, and the pillars that support that power. I also explained why it was absolutely critical that the commanders take what I said—and this briefing—and immediately communicate it back to their troops. Because this unit had already failed two nuclear surety inspections. Under Curtis LeMay's Strategic Air Command, one failure would have resulted in every commander on the base being fired. Nobody had been fired from this wing before I took over. So I had to lay the foundation that night.

The next morning, their task was simple: At every morning briefing, every shift briefing, all day long—communicate this very briefing. Explain what this culture means. Why it's important. Why their attention to detail must change—now.

Disciplined attention to detail meant three major categories of change:

1. Organizational changes.

2. Process changes.

3. Leader behavioral changes.

Organizationally, the first problem was that the wing I commanded didn't actually own the processes where the nuclear surety failures had occurred. Another organization on the base did. That organization—led by a different commander—handled nuclear weapons maintenance and handling. But we owned the failure.

So the first step in organizational change was for me to sit down with that other commander. I needed to learn about the failures—what went wrong—and get his perspective on what needed to change so these failures would never happen again. I didn't know every detail, but I understood the big picture. And so, that began the organizational change process.

If you look at the organization now, the commander who sits in the seat I once held now owns both organizations. They're fully integrated. He has direct command and control over the processes that matter most.

It took years to implement fully, well after I left. But it started under my watch. In the short term, the other commander and I conducted a full root cause analysis. We came up with an approach to put a band-aid on the organizational problems—something that would hold everything together and prevent another failure while the bigger changes were being worked out.

Now, as for leadership, you know the phrase "lead by example." That's not some throwaway cliche in my world. From the time I gave that speech, I was living it. On a day when most commanders would have taken the afternoon off and celebrated with their families, I was working in front of my commanders. Calling them in. Giving briefings. Sacrificing my afternoon off, demonstrating the discipline to work when I didn't have to—because this mission was more important.

One of the ways I got hands-on—and it drove some people crazy—is that we moved overnight from a hands-off commander to a hands-on, attention-to-detail, disciplined commander. Had I come in and, no matter what I said or did—even if I gave the right briefing—if I had just handed it out and said, "Hey, read this overnight. We'll get together later in the week to talk about it," it wouldn't have worked. That's hands-off. That's not how you fix a broken culture. That's why what I did that evening—the very evening I took command—mattered so much.

When I went to work for my first full day, I had already asked my emergency response team to prepare a no-notice nuclear emergency exercise inside the command post. This was a wargame for all the commanders and key decision-makers. Now, it wasn't a full-base exercise—it was a commander-level exercise with their immediate senior enlisted personnel.

Then began my reputation for being exceedingly detail-oriented. Then (and now), I ask pointed questions. I expect subordinates to be able to answer them, and clearly so. For instance, I do **not** accept it when someone talks around an answer but doesn't actually answer the question. That happens quite frequently in government—even in the military.

As I began training my commanders on the level of detail and discipline they were going to need in order to operate at my standard, the questions I asked weren't random; they were tools. My objective was to successfully conduct a nuclear emergency response operation—as flawlessly as humanly possible—and build in enough risk mitigation to prevent human error as close to 100 percent of the time as we could.

And that's how I started leading by example in the actual activity of the mission. Which cascaded out of that room, from that first event, through my entire seventeen months in command. And as a matter of fact, I would ultimately have the largest security forces operation in the Air Force—over 630 personnel. Upon my retirement, I received a special award plaque entitled, "Eye of the Tiger." Staff at my sending-off party played the song "Eye of the Tiger" and showed a video of me poking into their business daily—checking on their attention to detail and discipline.

This is all because I practiced something I learned as an enlisted kid: Lead by walking around. You see, I grew up in the Air Force as the son of a retired master sergeant. All of my mentors, when I was enlisted, taught me that real leadership means being present. You have to walk around and be seen. When you combine that leadership style with almost-obsessive detail-orientedness, well . . . let's just say I was cut out for this mission to fix things.

Sometimes walking took the form of driving. In the old Strategic Air Command days, the wing commander had a blue car with a white top. When I got there, they gave me a brand-new staff car, but it was just blue.

I said, "Put a white top on it."

The transportation people pushed back right away.

"Oh sir, no, we can't do that."

"Yes you can. Put a white top on it. I'm the wing commander. We're a nuclear organization. We're going to have a proper wing commander's car."

So they did. Now, when I was driving around, the older NCOs and commanders—those who remembered Strategic Air Command days—knew exactly who was coming when they saw that white-topped car. They taught that meaning to the younger people, especially the security forces who controlled everything— the gates, the fences, the facilities.

That's leadership by walking around.

Another such change I made right away was call signs. You've heard of Air Force One—that's just a call sign for any Air Force aircraft the president is aboard. Our unit emblem had a tiger on it. So, building pride and unity, I said, "Change my call sign to Tiger One."

Then I insisted all my commanders create their own call signs too. We published the list and built up unit morale right from the start.

So there I was, driving around in my blue car with the white top, with call sign Tiger One, showing up unexpectedly.

I would grab my senior enlisted guy—the Command Chief— and say, "Chief, at least three times a week, clear your schedule. We're going out."

At first, he was confused.

"Where are we going?"

"Wherever you think we need to go."

He caught on quick. Soon, he had locations ready every time. We didn't tell anyone we were coming. We just drove around and showed up.

It didn't take very long before the troops realized. *Colonel*

Maness is coming. And he's checking!

I only had to do a couple of field quizzes—grilling a young NCO or Airman with my level of detailed questions—before they figured it out to never be unprepared on the job.

Now, not everybody in the middle leadership ranks liked this. Some didn't want to change, so I added another tool. At my weekly staff meetings—about fifty people totaled up—I always brought in a young two-striper (a low-ranking airman) from a specific area. As someone who had been a nineteen-year-old sergeant, I knew: The youngest person in the room usually knows the most about what's really going on. And I was right. Time and time again, those young men and women would prove the mid-level leadership wrong.

I would ask,, "What do you think about what Colonel So-and-So just said?" or, "Chief So-and-So just said this. What's your perspective?"

And the young person would reveal the real picture. Fresh eyes can see old problems and talk about them; old eyes either can't see the problems anymore—or they see them and don't want to talk about them. Now, it's not strictly about age. A thirty-something who's new to the system can do it just as well. The point is, the younger or newer people are usually right there on the line, where things are actually happening. After all, leadership has a great span of control. At a place like this—53,000 acres, units spread out over miles and even mountain ranges—it's hard to be everywhere. The young men and women on the ground know what's happening. And if you listen carefully, you can even tell whether their mid-level leadership is spending time with them or not. And believe me . . . they don't mind complaining to the colonel if their bosses aren't doing their jobs!

But it didn't take long for everyone on base to do just that, their jobs. And do it right the first time. That one key mission-critical priority—disciplined attention to detail—very soon became a reality because I decided it first for myself, communicated it to those who would be responsible for following through when I wasn't there, led by example, and finally, expected excellence from all in my purview. Within ninety days of my taking command, we passed the nuclear surety inspection. (By the way, nuclear surety is a set of processes designed to guarantee the safety, security, and reliability of nuclear weapons. One element of nuclear surety is the two-person policy. That means no one is ever allowed to be alone in close proximity to a nuclear warhead. There must always be two authorized personnel present, to prevent any unintended—or intentional—actions that could lead to a nuclear detonation. I set the expectation of zero violations of the two-person policy. That shouldn't be hard to achieve if you're disciplined. If you're not, then it is.)

Beyond nuclear surety, I established specific goals such as, for example, "zero intrusions through the security perimeters protecting the nuclear weapons" and "zero violations of nuclear surety standards." Then I put timelines on training and certification for new personnel. Staff have to go through a process called the Personnel Reliability Program when they're brought into the nuclear weapons business. The program is intended for us to watch each other—peer monitoring. There are a *lot* of rules. For example, I couldn't even take an antihistamine pill without going to the doctor and reporting it because I was on the Personnel Reliability Program. We don't want anybody's mind or body being affected by medication we don't know about. That's mission-critical.

Naturally, I expected zero failures in that reporting process— meaning, if anything happened that would require someone to be pulled off nuclear weapons duty, it had to be reported properly every time. There's a whole host of metrics connected to that reporting. Top-level commanders and squadron commanders are directly involved. There's a non-commissioned officer that runs the program, usually at the squadron level. At my level, I was what's called the Certifying Official—responsible for the entire administration of the program. I was the final sign-off.

When someone was first accepted into the program—or if anyone directly under my command needed to be pulled off nuclear weapons duty for any reason—I had to be told. I had to make the decision to pull them. And then I had to make the decision to put them back on when the issue was resolved. But we had **zero errors**. Zero. None. None at all.

One more success to note: I also asked for a series of reviews of all operating technical data and checklists. As you might anticipate, there's a checklist for everything in the nuclear line of work—to make sure people follow the right steps, in the right order, with the right authorization. I expected zero errors here, too—and got just that.

That's how you build a system where people are doing the right tasks, at the right time, in the right way, by the right individuals. For seventeen straight months, we trained and exercised that constantly to make sure it happened. Security, administration, operations—it all had to line up perfectly. And it did.

Now, as a thought experiment, let's ask *What If?* What if I had recognized the issue—lax discipline—but missed what the vision was? Or had incompletely or incoherently communicated what the plan was? What if I had recognized the technical issues— resulting in the various security failures, for example—but missed setting the vision for what the culture needed to become?

Well, it would've been a disaster is what. Because what happens if you recognize technical problems, but you don't clearly articulate a vision and direction? You get reactive leadership. You get people who are just running around trying to fix problems as they pop up, instead of building a disciplined system that prevents problems before they occur.

If I had done that, if I had been overly worried, overly

focused on the events themselves—like, "Oh no, this inspector's coming! Oh no, this failure just happened!"—then it would've turned into a constant game of whack-a-mole. Every day would've been panic, trying to react to symptoms without ever addressing the root causes. The culture would have stayed broken. People would have hidden mistakes out of fear instead of learning to solve them early. And most importantly—the fundamental mission, the nuclear mission, would have stayed at risk. My heart could have been in the right place—fix the problems—but if we miss the vision, we're just reacting, not leading.

This is why we need all the things and in the right order: a new reality to be created, written in as few words as possible, and top-down to bottom-up commitment to implementing that new reality.

A TEMPLATE FOR CHANGE

Now, you might have noticed in my example a practical template to create massive change. It's pretty simple, actually.

- Find the root cause problem—and describe it in three to five words.

- Define the vision for the alternative you are going to launch.

- Communicate it to the people who can implement it, and those it affects.

- Get everyone in the room—literally or digitally—and communicate it all at once.

On that last point. Sometimes, it's a one-time meeting. Other times, it's perpetual—where you agitate on the topic consistently and keep casting the vision. You can say what it is you're standing for in three to five words—or in your case, four words. Then, you lay out:

- Here's what needs to change inside the organization.

- Here's what needs to change with the process.

- Here's what leading by example looks like.

By the way, on that last point? This can be self-appointed leadership—you don't have to wait until someone taps you on the shoulder. Of course, it can also be official—you're now in a position to change things because you've been put there. Either way, being reactionary and complaining doesn't work.

Here's how this process can look in action—so you go from worrying about *all* the problems out there to singularly focusing on *one* and absolutely blowing away the opposition.

THE FIRST THING TO DO FIRST: AN EXAMPLE

Consider this hypothetical example that is very real throughout the United States. Let's say you have an issue with your local school board bringing in so-called "banned books," which are basically just gay porn, into schools for children to consume. You, a parent in the school district, are very unhappy about this. Maybe your town is a more "purple" or blue-leaning area, and that's just how it goes around there, or the teachers are just doing whatever they want, regardless of what conservative parents in the district would have wanted.

So what would it look like to follow the approach of this chapter instead of simply being reactionary and complaining? Well, instead of simply saying, "We don't want this," and just demanding the books-be-gone, the question is: *What do you want instead?*

You decide this. And so maybe you address the school board. Maybe you address fellow parents. Maybe you organize a small community of parents, even if it's just a passionate minority. You lay out the vision for change. And you don't just say, "Don't do this. Get the books out." You say, "Here's what we want instead."

Remember what I said about **not** saying, "We're going to revert back to the original culture"? That's a key reason my effort was successful. I didn't frame it as reeducation (which sounds communist anyway). I instead laid out the culture we needed, without the nostalgia. I just put the end state out there—what success looks like.

The same thing applies here. Maybe you start with a little complaining, sure—in the city newspaper op-ed, maybe—but even there, you have to provide a solution. It can't stop at complaints. That's your opening salvo, but it has to lead to action, with simple, positive framing.

In this hypothetical, instead of just saying "Take back the schools and libraries," you have to be clear. Maybe your three-to-five-word solution is, "Let Parents Decide." It's simple, positive, and powerful. In this very real situation happening across the country, parents are generally just complaining. Because the Right tends to be "leave me alone and let me live my life." The Left isn't like that. Their ideas are so unpopular that they have to recruit. They have to engage in what I'd call ideological press gangs, like the way the British Navy used to conscript sailors. So they target the most vulnerable. That's how their movement survives.

Anyway, instead of shouting, "Get gay porn out of libraries and schools," you go for something positive. Like, "Let Parents Decide," or perhaps even, "Parents' Bill of Rights." Both are universally, unassailably positive. So if anyone opposes it, they're saying parents shouldn't have rights over their children's education—a truly unpopular position to hold!

And then, either you become the leadership yourself, or you persuade leadership to join you. If they won't listen, you run for the school board yourself. Then it becomes about campaign fundamentals. Either way, the majority are on your side, and more importantly, you speak for them. Your vision is theirs now, and vice-versa. No more reactionary complaints, only building real alternatives here.

Since leaving the military I've seen America's culture be chipped away at by communists embedded within our own society and I'm not surprised. Every step I take today to influence my community, or the government is about cultural change. Yes, the communists have always known they couldn't defeat us on the battlefield but could if they destroy our culture from within. Only a few generations of American school children have to be indoctrinated if society doesn't recognize the attack and take actions to stop it.

CHAPTER 6

Model the Great Men of History to Become a Good One

My father—MSgt Billy Maness—along with my uncles Buddy, Clyde, Leon, George, Billy, Charlie, Bobby, and Tom, and my first Air Force boss, SMSgt Jim Powlas, all had a major influence on me. Most of them had military experience as non-commissioned officers, and many were farmers or public school teachers, or both. They provided the core of my being, the foundation that made me the kind of person who could seek out, study, and appreciate timeless examples of courageous leadership. As a little kid, I remember overhearing my dad and uncles naming the great names of history when we'd "visit" (that's the Southern way to say, have someone over to your house, provide a little hospitality, and talk about matters of some significance). Men that came up often enough for me to remember them by the time

I could read were Alexander the Great, George Washington, and the Kennedys. Obviously not all Americans, but when I began to read, I chose biographies of theirs, which would shape my own thinking—and doing.

One thing I learned along the way: Be careful. Just reading history about a person doesn't always give you the full picture. That's why, wherever I could, I tried to go deeper. I looked for the individual's own writing—primary documents—to get a real sense of who they actually were, not just how history books chose to present them.

THE GREAT MEN OF HISTORY, ABRIDGED EDITION

When I was growing up in the 1960s, all my elders were all **President John F. Kennedy** voters and even fans. Though he was assassinated when I was about two years old, I heard a lot about him throughout my childhood. In death, he lived larger than life. Naturally, I read quite a bit about him, too. The first I ever read about Kennedy was the story of PT-109. August 1st through 7th, 1943, then-Lieutenant John Kennedy of the United States Navy saved the lives of ten other sailors after their watercraft was destroyed by a Japanese vessel. The ensuing adventure— swimming for miles in open ocean, surviving on coconuts, evading the enemy in spite of injured comrades—is the stuff of Hollywood. The story also brought Kennedy into the public eye; we would never from that point on look away.

Between him and his brother **Robert**, their stories fascinated me. I know they were Democrats, but honestly, those two—John and brother Robert Kennedy, Senior—had a lasting influence on me. When I first ran for Senate, a Republican supporter gave me a copy of *The Last Campaign*, which tells the story of Robert

Kennedy's presidential campaign—the one during which he was ultimately assassinated, like his brother before him. I toted that book around with me while driving through Louisiana in my truck, making calls and meeting potential donors to raise money the old-fashioned way. And I was surprised when I read it—pleasantly surprised. Reading about Robert's thinking, and John's, too, I realized how similar my own views were to theirs. Especially their policy thinking. They were, in a word, Americanists. I don't believe they would be Democrats today, by any stretch. Their worldview shaped me more than I realized, even before I read *The Last Campaign* cover to cover during my 2014 run.

Beyond the Kennedys, I was an avid reader of biographies, always drawn to stories of leadership and challenge.

Alexander the Great was another figure who caught my attention, though in a different way. Now, I haven't read anything directly written by Alexander himself; I don't even know if anything like that exists. But what stood out to me about him came from reading secondary sources, likely one of those old biography series for kids they used to publish. It made a real impression.

Before I joined the military, when I was about fifteen or sixteen, I was trying to decide if I really wanted to pursue that path. I had always dreamed of being a fighter pilot, but I also wanted to become a commander, a real leader. I officially started out in the military at age seventeen. That was the first hurdle: *Could I even do this at my age?* The day I showed up for basic training, I weighed 115 pounds, stood 5'10", and was the youngest person in my basic training flight.

In the Air Force, we don't call them platoons and companies like they do in the Army. We have flights, squadrons, groups, wings. Being the youngest guy in my flight, I had to think seriously about whether I belonged there. Around that time, I had read about Alexander the Great—this young man who, at an even younger age than me, led armies and built an empire. A few things about him stuck with me: his youth, the caliber of the teachers he had, and his ability to make incredibly sophisticated strategic decisions at such a young age. One decision in particular stood out; this was his choice *not* to try to conquer the region we now know as Afghanistan. Even back then, it was called "the graveyard of empire" for a reason. Alexander understood something most leaders twice his age would have missed—the high cost and low reward of trying to dominate that particular territory.

The fact that a young man could have that level of foresight was remarkable to me. It showed that leadership included more than courage or charisma but also clarity. Great leaders do *not* let their egos drag them into unwinnable fights. That was the kind of commander I wanted to be.

As I moved through my career in the military, I would constantly go back and remind myself about him. He was very young, but also very good—because he studied hard and had been taught well. I think instinctively, because I had read about men like Alexander, I sought out mentors. I wanted the kind of training and education that would help me succeed, too.

Honestly, my most valuable education didn't necessarily come from the institutions I attended. It came from the people I met along the way who became mentors. That approach—don't focus on your youth and inexperience; study hard and seek out the right people—served me well from the very beginning.

Growing up, another figure who stood out to me was **George Washington**. I first came across him like most kids did—reading a biography written for schoolchildren. It was the usual story: chopping down the cherry tree, being unfailingly honest, the patriotic icing on top of a pretty simple cake. Later, though, what really caught my interest were three particular sets of facts.

First, Washington's public reputation. I read some writings from people who knew him personally, describing how Washington behaved in public. He lived out his own *Washington's Rules of*

Civility. I still have my copy to this day. I read it as a teenager and again later on, and when I put it together with what I had already learned about him, it all made sense. The way he interacted with people—the manners, the self-discipline, the respect he showed others—left a real impression. His actions, not just his words, set the tone. That's why I gave a copy of *Rules of Civility* to each of my kids. It's a standard worth aiming for, for all of us.

The second thing that struck me about Washington's special character was from a professional perspective. Washington wasn't necessarily the smartest man in the room. Think about it . . . at Independence Hall, he was surrounded by some of the greatest minds the colonies had to offer. Yet, it wasn't raw intellect that set him apart; it was character. Courage. Manners. Common sense. The ability to disagree without tearing people down. True care for his fellow man.

Now, I've been in a lot of rooms with very smart people in my career, and I've never been the smartest guy in the room. In a room full of the greatest minds in the colonies—Jefferson, Adams, Franklin—Washington wasn't necessarily the most brilliant. But he was the man of the greatest character. When I say character, I mean courage, manners, steadiness, humility. The ability to disagree without tearing someone down. A true care for his fellow man. He brought those traits to every room he entered, and that's why he was trusted with the future of the country.

That said, the greatest act of leadership Washington ever made—and maybe the greatest act of any military leader in history—was giving up his commission as commander-in-chief after the war was over. He returned it to Congress.

That decision, that selfless act, is why we have a Republic today, even with all our problems. Without that moment, America could easily have slid into a military dictatorship or a new monarchy. Washington chose to walk away from absolute power. As someone who's worn the uniform and commanded troops, I understand just how much courage—and sacrifice—that took. It's easy to praise selflessness. It's much harder to actually live it out close to 100 percent of the time, in every situation. Washington did.

Third and finally, Washington also brought real-world skills to America's table. He had military experience as a Virginia militia colonel, and he was a surveyor by trade. That little biographical detail of Washington's has always stuck with me, too—probably because one of my own personal heroes growing up was my Uncle Tom. He had served in Patton's Army during World War II as a tank machine gunner, and after the war, became a surveyor and eventually a three-term County Highway Commissioner. Uncle Tom's surveying career led to some of my favorite childhood memories, like going hunting with him in West Tennessee. I'll never forget being with him when we killed the bobcat that's still on display in my aunt's living room today along with the stuffed owl from another hunt. Those experiences connected me in a small but meaningful way to the kind of life George Washington lived before he ever commanded men or founded the nation. It was Washington's skills as a land surveyor that first carried him across the frontier, opened doors for him, and prepared him for everything that followed. Surveying led him to travel widely as a young man, especially to the Western frontier. It gave him a perspective most people never had, a literal ground-level view of the new land and its challenges. And like my Uncle Tom, my Uncle Charlie was also a surveyor; he ran bridge construction projects for the state highway department as well. That's the American way: studying the land, then building over it, from young surveyor George Washington to President Eisenhower's interstate highway projects.

Earlier, I wrote a little about **Davy Crockett**, but his story merits another mention. Crockett resonates with me because his life mirrored the people I knew best growing up—my family, my neighbors, the folks of West Tennessee. My dad's people migrated over from western North Carolina in the early 1800s and settled in West Tennessee. So when I read about Crockett, I saw my grandpa, my uncles, my brothers, myself. The fierce independence. The refusal to say "I can't." That stubborn streak of self-reliance . . . it's in all of us down there, sometimes to a fault.

I first read about Crockett when I was a little kid. My aunt, who was a schoolteacher, gave me a biography of him, and one of Daniel Boone, too. But what set Crockett apart for me, though, was his willingness to push back against power, even against someone like President Andrew Jackson. Jackson was another figure I admired, so at first you'd think they'd be natural allies. They were, early on, but when Jackson pushed for the forced relocation of the Cherokee people, Crockett stood up and opposed him. That took guts. It cost him politically. But he stood on principle. And I admire that.

Now, a few words about **Andrew Jackson** himself. The first story of his I ever read was about when he was just fourteen years old, fighting in the American Revolution. He was captured by the British, beaten badly, but survived. He kept fighting.

Jackson's whole life is a story of overcoming obstacles. He became a lawyer without going to law school, apprenticing instead. He didn't come from privilege; he worked for everything he had. Same with his military career. It wasn't a straight shot to success. He had failures and setbacks. But he kept going, kept fighting.

So it's not Jackson's policies that lead me to admire him—although I do think he was a better president than historians give him credit for. It's who he was: a man who saw obstacles and figured out a way through them. In this way, Andrew Jackson shares similarity with Donald J. Trump. Both men fought the establishment, both were hated by the elites, and both were willing to take punches and keep swinging.

Next on the list, we have probably the most controversial figure: **Jefferson Davis**. His last home—where he lived after the

American Civil War—is just down the road from my house on Mississippi's Gulf of America coast. It's called Beauvoir, and there's a presidential library there, too—small, but beautiful—and is actually funded in part by US federal tax dollars. On the grounds is the "Arlington Cemetery of the Confederacy," as it's called. Of special note is the Confederate Army's Tomb of the Unknown Soldier. Davis's own father is buried there, too; he was a Continental Army veteran of the American Revolution. I picked up my copy of *The Rise and Fall of the Confederate Government*, the history Davis wrote about the Confederacy, at the Beauvoir gift shop.

It may surprise you, growing up in the American South, that I didn't hear or read much about Jefferson Davis as a kid. Growing up in Tennessee, you get taught the basic American history: *The Civil War was about slavery; the South seceded because of slavery.* That's pretty much it. But when I got to college, in freshman year, I had to write an English paper. Now, I didn't write it about Davis; I wrote about why Thomas Jefferson wasn't able to get the abolition of slavery into the Declaration of Independence. In that research, I came across Jefferson Davis's name. A lot.

Which confused me, honestly. Because when you start digging into primary documents—reading what American antebellum influencers actually wrote and said—it gets a lot more complicated. Yes, slavery was there. It was the fuel, the combustible material, behind secession. There is no denying that. But if you take a step back, you realize the real engine, that which drove the secession crisis, was the Constitution. Specifically, the original relationship between the states and the federal government—and the division of power between them.

The more I read from Jefferson Davis—not just *about* him— the more I realized that once we set aside the surface-level history we're usually taught, the deeper, *truer* story emerges. Maybe these guys—Jefferson Davis and other Confederates—really *were* trying to "support and defend the Constitution," as they understood it. Because they were willing to risk everything for it.

Of course, the Union won the American Civil War, and the victors get to write the history books. That's how it always works. But when you look at Davis through a different lens—*his* lens— you see a man who stood up for what he believed in. From his perspective, the War Between the States was fought over whether the states had entered into this compact voluntarily—and whether they should be able to leave it voluntarily when the compact was broken by the federal government or by other states.

From the Confederacy's perspective, the Union—meaning the federal government—had dramatically overreached its power. The federal government had become ultra-federalist at the expense of the individual states' right to decide for themselves what would and would not be allowed. And one of those issues was slavery, of course. But again, the real constitutional issue wasn't simply slavery itself. It boiled down to this: *Can a citizen of a state take his legally recognized personal property into the federal territories, just like every other citizen can?*

Indeed, slaves were treated as personal property under the law at that time. And the federal government passed laws— particularly concerning the Northwest Territories—that said a person who owned slaves could **not** take that property into those territories. That, naturally, created a problem: *Am I, as a citizen of, say, Mississippi, no longer allowed to move freely throughout the United States with my lawful property? Doesn't the Constitution guarantee that right—to move across state lines and settle anywhere inside the Union?*

That was the grievance. Thinking on it today, we know it's terrible because the property in question was human beings. There's no getting around how morally wrong that was. Everybody knew it, too, including Southerners. The United States had already placed limits on the slave trade early on. In the Constitution itself, there's a clause that set a deadline for when Congress bans the international slave trade. And on the very first day they were allowed to, Congress passed that ban, in 1807. The founding generation understood slavery was wrong, but it was tangled up in every part of the economy and society at the time, north and south.

That's what made it so hard: The constitutional issue of rights and state sovereignty gets wrapped up with the horrific reality of slavery. And when you separate the legal-constitutional issue from the moral one—when you understand the core political grievance—you realize that, in their own minds, many Southerners genuinely believed they were defending the original Constitution.

If you could sit across the table from Jefferson Davis, or from any of the governors or senators or state legislators of the time, you would hear that from them directly. Davis himself had been in the US senate for years during the major debates over these questions.

The bottom line is, from Davis's perspective, the Constitution—the compact between the states—was being disassembled. The states had entered into it voluntarily, giving up some of their sovereignty to the central government voluntarily. And there was no law saying that a state couldn't leave voluntarily. In fact, in the early days of the Union, some northeastern states had seriously discussed seceding. Legal opinion at the time said it would not have been unconstitutional for them to do so. So from the very beginning of the Union, the right of secession was debated—and never definitively settled.

When you look at the Confederates through that lens, you realize they had a point.

Unfortunately, the point was wrapped up in slavery, and that's the part people understandably struggle with. And we should struggle with it. Now, we also have to get to the facts—the true legal and constitutional decisions that were made, and the multiple, overlapping factors that drove them. The federal government had become too powerful for the southern states' own good, they believed. I have a personal story about that.

A few years ago, over in Louisiana, I got to play a small part on the team—Democrats and Republicans together—that did away with the last Jim Crow law still on the books in the United States. It was a law allowing non-unanimous juries, passed back in the 1890s or so. I was proud to be on that team. Even though we eliminated the non-unanimous jury law, there are still over a hundred people—maybe more—who were convicted under it and haven't been given any appellate relief yet. So I was asked to write a letter of support for Senate Bill 218 in May 2025, which was just introduced in the Louisiana legislature, as of this writing; I wrote that letter of support the same week I wrote this chapter. The bill would provide that relief and finally put the issue to bed for good.

That original effort was a big deal down in Louisiana. The law was still active all the way up to 2018. I think what you're referencing is right—there was a proposal under the "Ending Jim Crow Juries" initiative. That's what we were a part of.

The way I got involved was through a friend of mine named Ed Tarpley, a former prosecutor in Alexandria, Louisiana. He was leading the team. I ran into them at the legislature one day—they were there lobbying for support—and that's how I joined the effort. Ed and I had gotten to know each other during my Senate races.

The final push to get rid of non-unanimous jury decisions was a state constitutional amendment, passed by the voters after going through the legislature. Eventually, the Supreme Court ruled on it, too, and outlawed it across the board. But as of now, there are still about 773 people in prison due to non-unanimous jury convictions.

Now, the law may indeed date to the Jim Crow era, but it wasn't only black people who were affected. I got involved in the criminal justice reform movement—not the extreme version, but the kind that someone like President Trump has supported—well before our President became an advocate. What inspired me was the prison population numbers in Louisiana: With an incarceration rate of 1,067 per 100,000 residents, Louisiana locks up a higher percentage of its people than just about anywhere else[5]. We are basically creating more and more career criminals, especially in the black community. And that has ripple effects—robbing kids of their dads, fueling generational poverty, and keeping the cycle going. So I started supporting moderate reforms and policies that might throw a wrench into that system, to disrupt it somehow.

You haven't really lived until you've visited the prison in Angola, Louisiana. That's the "lifer" prison; If you're sent to Angola, it's because you've got a life sentence. It's where they hold the famous prison rodeo. Movies have been made about it. I've been there several times over the years, mostly for political reasons—campaigning, yes, but also to observe and support some of the programs they're doing in there.

One of the most powerful things they do is bring in young black men—some under twenty-five, some a bit older—who don't have any real skills training. They bring them into Angola temporarily for two reasons. First, to give them actual training in HVAC, electrical work, and other trades. Johnson Controls runs one of the programs. The second reason is even more important— they pair them with lifers for mentorship. These guys serving life sentences get trained to be instructors and mentors. They tell their stories and try to steer the younger guys away from repeating their mistakes. It's powerful; it gives both sides something meaningful. The lifers get to contribute, and the kids get a shot at a different future.

Angola's also a working farm, and if you've seen those old

---

5   Prison Policy Initiative, "Louisiana Profile," Prison Policy Initiative, accessed April 21, 2026, https://www.prisonpolicy.org/profiles/LA.html.

movies where prisoners are out working fields or digging ditches on a chain gang, those were shot at Angola. It's like a small country. When someone dies there, they don't leave. They're buried on the grounds, taken to the grave in a glass-sided horse-drawn hearse. The caskets are made by the prisoners themselves.

When you actually sit down and talk to someone who's been through that system—and you see it firsthand—you realize something: There was no way out for them. There never was. Not even in death do you get out. From the very beginning, the path the Angola inmates are on was laid out. Society hadn't recognized the issue back then. From a racial and cultural standpoint, there weren't any guardrails to keep them from ending up in prison.

Once you talk to inmates, you realize it's the right thing to do to make sure our system does a couple of things. First, we've got to break that cycle of career criminality. In Louisiana especially, it's a black male issue. When fathers are taken out of families and locked up, it leads to generational damage; nearly 70 percent of all Black babies in America today are born to unmarried mothers, and 64 percent of all Black children grow up in a single-parent home[6]. That wasn't always the case. During my campaign, when I started digging into this (because one needs to know everything he can about his possible future constituents), I spoke with sheriffs, police, and leaders in the community—including black supporters. We all agreed on one big thing: Too many young black men are being locked up, and the system is highly effective at doing it. Now, yes, some of them are guilty—no question about it. But many were convicted under that non-unanimous jury process. In Louisiana, you could go to trial and be convicted by a split jury for nearly *everything* short of a capital crime. And while that didn't only

---

6   Jack Brewer and Alveda King, "Op-Ed: This Black History Month Let's Shine a Spotlight on Fatherlessness and Saving Black Babies," *America First Policy Institute,* February 1, 2023, https://americafirstpolicy.com/issues/op-ed-this-black-history-month-lets-shine-a-spotlight-on-fatherlessness-and-saving-black-babies.

affect black people, in practice, it did hit that community harder.

A big part of the problem came from that 1994 crime bill then-Senator Biden pushed through. That bill introduced automatic sentencing, like three-strikes laws. The way it was written triggered a massive prison population boom. That was the system I was staring at when I first ran for office. That said, just because a system may result in more black or Hispanic men being incarcerated doesn't automatically mean the system is "systemically racist." There may be a racial impact, but that doesn't mean racism was baked into the design. There are a lot of factors at play.

What I've focused on is making sure the system works fairly. Even if someone's accused of a crime—even if they're guilty—the system has to be just, or it doesn't work at all. That's the line I've always walked. We've got to be able to say: "Yes, let's keep dangerous people behind bars. But let's also fix what's broken and stop throwing people away when we know there's a better path forward."

By the way, this is why I'm 100 percent pro-life; I no longer advocate for the death penalty. You see, if a government is going to be given the power to take a life as punishment, then that government must be able to implement, maintain, and carry out that process without error—ever. Not one innocent person can be killed in that kind of system. And the truth is, it has happened enough times.

That's where I landed on the issue—and my wife, Candy, did too. We're both very conservative, staunchly pro-life, but for years we weren't opposed to the death penalty. I wouldn't say I was "pro" death penalty, but I never took a stand against it, not actively. I just assumed it was one of those necessary tools of justice. But at a certain point we looked at each other and said, "You know what? We don't think the government is capable of implementing the death penalty without making mistakes."

There have been enough documented, proven cases—real

ones, not just technicalities or lucky breaks for the convict—where someone was wrongfully sentenced to death. That's enough.

There was a man up in Shreveport—a black man on death row—named Glenn Ford. Eventually, new evidence came to light, and he was released, but only after he had been diagnosed with terminal lung cancer. The state of Louisiana never acknowledged this mistake to any sufficient extent. No apology. No compensation for what they took from him. Glenn spent twenty-nine years, three months, and five days in solitary confinement, only to live fewer than sixteen months a free man again.

That case stuck with us—especially because my wife was going through her own cancer diagnosis at the time. That breast cancer diagnosis was one of the main reasons I left the Air Force when I did, by the way; I needed to be there for her. So when we saw that wrongfully convicted gentleman's story, it hit home. It forced us to talk through something we'd never fully sorted out: *How we could be pro-life but still support a system that, even once, might take an innocent life?*

So we came to a new conviction—one we now share completely: If you're truly pro-life, you have to be consistent. We don't believe in exceptions to that principle. Not for rape. Not for the death penalty (because the child didn't commit the crime, in the case of post-rape abortion). The government simply cannot be trusted to get it right every time. And if the government can't do it right, it shouldn't do it at all.

Now, continuing the subject of government overreach, then and now, consider President Abraham Lincoln's speeches before the Civil War. This was an issue in the 1850s just as it is today—the government takes power it does not deserve. In any case, President Lincoln outright said, multiple times, that he had no interest in using military force against the states that seceded. He said he had no constitutional power to do so. Yet he did anyway; he used force and violence to hold the Union together—a move that was far beyond the president's powers under the Constitution at the time. The Union's invasion of the southern states in 1861 was, in effect, a mass-death penalty for what was not even unconstitutional, much less illegal: secession And what happened because of it?

Today, we live in a surveillance state run by a centralized federal government that exercises powers the founders never dreamed of. Federal law enforcement agents now routinely wield authority never granted to them by the Constitution. During COVID-19, I saw firsthand that the government could simply decide to restrict my movement across state lines. All of this—the massive federal overreach, the surveillance, the censorship—you can trace back to steps taken by Abraham Lincoln during the Civil War.

There's a book by my friend Mike Church entitled *What Lincoln Killed*. Its argument is simple: Lincoln set the precedent for a central government that could do whatever it pleased, constitutional limits be damned. It didn't all happen at once. As always, history is complicated, with multiple factors at work. But the thread runs straight from Lincoln's decisions in 1861 to the surveillance state we live under today. No doubt about it.

Alright, let's fast forward a few decades now. And sail an ocean. Let's meet **Winston Churchill** in his prime.

The thing that draws me to him is what I learned while I was at Harvard. I read part one of *The Last Lion* while I was there. Of course, I knew who Churchill was. I grew up during the Cold War. I knew about the "Iron Curtain" speech. I knew he'd been Prime Minister during World War II . . . the basic stuff every "normie" knows about him. But what I didn't know until then was that he had been a failure.

Because of his family, Churchill went into the military, and he was successful there as a young officer. He had physical courage and made good decisions under fire. He fought in India, the Sudan, and in the Boer War. There's some propaganda around each of those events, so it's hard to separate postimperial myth from biographical fact. The point is, Churchill carried himself well as a soldier. But as a politician, though? He failed, over and over again.

He was in the political wilderness for decades, right up until Neville Chamberlain screwed up with the infamous appeasement of Adolf Hitler. Even when Churchill was finally picked to replace Chamberlain as Prime Minister, this was controversial. People doubted him. They thought maybe this was a mistake. It was not.

Had I not known Churchill's story, I don't think I ever would've been a commander in the U.S. Air Force. Because my experience leading up to my own command was the same: Until the moment I took the flag in my hands and accepted command of a squadron, I didn't really believe they were going to let me do it.

And I get the sense, from everything I've read about Churchill, he felt the same way. He didn't really believe they were going to trust him with that level of responsibility. But when they did, he took it and ran with it.

Now, after the war, Churchill lost power immediately. Lost his seat, lost the Prime Ministership—gone. He did come back for one more term, the highlight of which was the Iron Curtain speech, warning the world about the Soviet Union. Still, what a story. Churchill had absolutely zero power until the day he was handed power because of a national crisis. And once the crisis ended, that power was taken away almost immediately.

That's the story of Churchill—a man who was ready when the moment came, even if the moment almost never came. And he's probably the greatest leader England has ever produced.

On a lighter note, a few years ago, I started drinking scotch every once in a while. Thanks, old Winnie.

A contemporary of Churchill was **President Harry Truman**—an average American until he very much was not. He was just a dude with a hat and glasses. A little guy. And I was little growing up, too, and sickly for a while. So when I would see Harry Truman—just a little man from Missouri, looking like anybody's grandpa—I thought, *If he can become President of the United States, I can do anything.* That's my very first memory of my very first thought about Harry Truman.

My grandparents were all Democrats, so there were pictures of FDR, John F. Kennedy, and Harry Truman hanging around their homes. That's where (and how) I first got to know these names. Years later, when I went to Harvard, I had a classmate named Mike Hill. He was the research assistant for David McCullough's biography *Truman,* which came out right around that time, in 1995.

Mike and I spent a lot of time together—and drank a lot of beer together at John Harvard's Pub which was right off Harvard Yard. And what struck me as interesting about Truman, from talking to Mike and then reading McCullough's book, was just how ordinary he really was. That's exactly my impression of him as a child hearing my elders tell his story from time to time. He wasn't a wildly successful businessman. He was a pretty average artillery officer in World War I.

But he deeply, genuinely loved his wife and daughter. You can see it over and over again in his letters.

Another thing that stood out about Truman—and this hit close to home for me—was that he learned roads. County roads. Remember my Uncle Tom, the county highway commissioner? Close to home, for me. Truman got his political start knowing the roads of Missouri better than anybody. That sticks with you. It's practical knowledge, real-world knowledge. Truman knew that if you wanted to fix something, if you wanted to build something, if you wanted to help people—you started with the roads.

Along the way, Truman found a political mentor, the "boss" of Kansas City politics, Thomas Pendergast. That relationship launched Truman's political career—first as a senator, then, by pure happenstance, as Vice President. When FDR died in office, Truman became President. And in no time at all, he was faced with the biggest decision any President of the United States has ever had to make: whether to drop the atomic bomb . . . or not.

Now, I've read about it, I've talked with Mike Hill about it, and I've dug into the primary sources at the Truman Library. Here's what the facts show:

The intelligence said if we invaded Japan conventionally, we were looking at over a million Allied casualties—most of them American—and likely a million dead Japanese civilians, too. Why? Well, the Japanese weren't going to surrender. They were ready to throw themselves into the fight, every man, woman, and child. And the Russians were *not* going to help, except to sweep in at the last minute and take the credit (and any spoils they could). It would have been total devastation. So had I been faced with that same decision, knowing what President Truman knew, I believe I would have made the same call.

Now, did Truman really understand the full devastation an atomic bomb would unleash? I don't think anybody truly did. Even the scientists behind it—Robert Oppenheimer, even Albert Einstein—had theoretical ideas, but nobody had ever seen the theory put into practice. Not until it happened.

Later in my career, I flew with Paul Tibbets IV—the grandson of the man who dropped the first atomic bomb, Paul Tibbets, commander of the 509th Bomb Group and the pilot of the aircraft, the Enola Gay, that dropped that very first atomic bomb. Through his grandson—whom I had the privilege of flying with in B-1 bombers—I eventually met the original Paul Tibbets, twice. (Paul Tibbets IV went on to command the 509th Bomb Wing at Whiteman Air Force Base, which is the modern descendant of the same bomb group that Tibbets' Enola Gay flew with during World War II.) Now, both times I met the elder Paul Tibbets—and these meetings were about five years apart—I asked him if he had any regrets about dropping the atomic bomb on Hiroshima. Both times, he looked me dead in the eye and said, "Hell no. It was the right thing to do then. It would be the right thing to do right now. None of the guys on my crew had any regrets either, no matter what the media has written about us."

I believe him.

Now, here's something those who whine about the atomic bomb never bring up: Curtis LeMay—who commanded the 20th Air Force in the Pacific—had already launched wave after wave of B-29s carrying incendiary bombs. We had firebombed Tokyo. We had firebombed dozens of other Japanese cities. And we had killed far more people with conventional bombing than we ever did at Hiroshima or Nagasaki. Now, Japanese cities were constructed primarily of wood. And with Lemay's bombing runs, firestorms raced through the neighborhoods, incinerating men, women, children. It was slow. It was horrifying. It was inhumane. And yet the public generally doesn't even blink about the firebombing, all while Hiroshima and Nagasaki get endlessly re-litigated. The cold, uncomfortable truth is, the atomic bomb was quicker. If you had to die one way or the other—being instantly vaporized in an atomic blast, or slowly burned alive in an incendiary inferno— which would you choose?

And yet the atomic bomb was so significant in comparison, the treacherous Rosenbergs stole the plans for the Soviets. And that's how we ultimately find ourselves at our next great American, **Ronald Reagan.** I got to meet President Reagan a couple times; I was part of the EOD—Explosive Ordnance Disposal—teams that augmented the Secret Service protective details. (The Secret Service doesn't have its own bomb disposal technicians, so they pull military guys like us into the operation. We'd work undercover, dressed in civilian suits, screening vehicles, buildings, parade routes. One time, I got to search "The Beast"—the Presidential limousine—before Reagan climbed in after attending Richard Petty's last race at Daytona.)

What's most notable about Reagan is that he was a

professional actor. At first, that's all I thought about him. *Well, yeah, of course he's a great communicator. He's acting.* But the more I studied him, I came to realize he wasn't acting. His vision was genuine. He understood the idea of America—the idea of liberty, private property, individual dignity—better than almost anyone in politics. But because he was an actor, he could *dramatize* that idea; he could bring it to life in a way ordinary politicians never could. He believed in his role; he *lived* his role. When he spoke about America—about the shining city on a hill—you could feel that it wasn't scripted.

Now at this point, you probably have a question. I know I would. So What?

Exactly. How does all this prepare you for the unexpected? For "what you can do about it"—and what you feel you *must* do about it?

Well, heroic American leadership is beyond integrity. Though integrity matters. Becoming the person who is capable of great change means knowing yourself. Knowing your strengths. Knowing your flaws. Understanding where you're likely to overreact, where you're likely to hesitate, where you're vulnerable. When you're presented with a total unknown—a moment that blindsides you— if you know yourself well enough, you can react faster, smarter, with greater clarity. You can also look back and understand why you reacted the way you did, and you can grow from it.

Over time, you start to recognize your own flaws ahead of time. You prepare yourself internally for those moments when the unexpected happens. No, it's never perfect. But it's better than being caught flat-footed with no idea who you really are.

And you can learn **all** of that through your own experience, but **first** you can learn it through the experiences of others whose successes are worth emulating—and their failures, avoiding them. That said, wrapped up in all this talk about great men in history is **courage**.

COURAGE, COWARDICE, AND LESSONS FROM COVID-19

When we're young, we think courage is the kind Davy Crockett showed at the Alamo. Physical courage. Facing bullets and bayonets. But I've come to realize the hardest kind of courage is moral courage. The courage to make the right call—not in the face of gunfire, but in the face of peer pressure. In the face of government oppression. Of public ridicule. The kind of courage it takes to tell a group of young men and women to go do something you know may get them killed—because it's necessary for the mission, for the cause, for the country.

Moral courage is harder than physical courage. It's much rarer, too. Just think about the last few years. Specifically, look at the COVID-19 pandemic response. The generals. The admirals. The senior civilians in government. How many of them showed moral courage? How many of them stood up when people's liberties were being suppressed? When bad decisions were being made at the expense of Americans' lives and rights? Very few. Most failed. Went along. Kept their mouths shut to protect their careers. And when a few brave ones did stand up, they were axed one way or another—quietly pushed out or publicly destroyed.

The worst atrocity was the order to impose the vaccine mandate on military personnel, which was objectively unconstitutional and illegal. Yet how many generals and admirals obeyed that unlawful order? How many enforced it on young men and women anyway, ruining careers, breaking trust, damaging morale?

The difference between those who failed and those who stood firm was moral courage. The hardest courage. The rarest courage. The kind of courage America desperately needs right now from all of us.

The military vaccine mandate—and the overt and implicit

defenses of it by the top brass—remains the most devastating failure of moral courage I've ever seen in my life. *They were protecting the institution instead of protecting the Constitution.*

And that phenomenon is *still* happening across the military post-COVID, and in the intelligence community—at the FBI, the NSA, the CIA. At every level of government and law enforcement where people took an oath to protect and defend the Constitution of the United States. Instead of protecting the Constitution, they're protecting their institutions. Because those institutions—and the networks, the leadership, the promotion ladders—are what built them. What gave them their power, their prestige, their status. So they're not defending the law; they're defending what "made" them.

There's a whole movement now trying to fight back against this and enforce accountability. I'm part of it, specifically, the Declaration of Military Accountability[7]. There are 231 individuals who signed it originally and almost 40,000 have signed it at this point; I'm the most senior officer who has signed. The letter demands righteous justice for, among other things, those who've suffered "debilitating vaccine injuries" due to military leadership who "broke the law."

We tried to get retired generals and admirals to stand with us, but not a single one would sign. Not one. That should tell you everything you need to know about the moral rot at the top levels of our institutions today.

I told the young people who signed the Declaration of Military Accountability—those who stood up and fought back against unlawful orders during the COVID era, "Honestly, guys, I don't know if I would've been able to do what you have done. But I'm supporting you. That's why I'm putting my name on this."

---

7   U.S. House of Representatives, Committee on Oversight and Accountability, "Declaration of Military Accountability: An Open Letter to the American People," January 11, 2024, https://www.congress.gov/118/meeting/house/116730/documents/HHRG-118-GO06-20240111-SD003.pdf.

When I was Vice Wing Commander at Offutt Air Force Base in Omaha, Nebraska, one of my responsibilities was pandemic planning. We came close to a flu pandemic that particular year. It didn't happen, but we war-gamed it and ran exercises. We brought in local, city, county, and state leaders to coordinate.

One of the things I learned was that the military had a plan to control the distribution of medications if there was ever a shortage. That struck me as interesting—even a little alarming—but it was treated like just another logistics problem. We were focused on nuts and bolts: how to get vaccines and medications into local communities, how to coordinate logistics, how to secure shipments moving from civilian airports to military bases, and what to do if convoys were attacked by panicked civilians.

It felt like a blip. It didn't happen. We moved on. But I remember even back then, during the planning sessions, some of us said quietly to each other, "This feels a little heavy-handed," using military-like forced obedience as the way to respond to disease. We assumed it wouldn't come to that. We assumed it was just a contingency. But looking back now, after living through COVID-19, I realize we had no idea how deep the instinct to suppress individual rights ran across every level of government. Even that little glimpse into pandemic planning hadn't prepared me for the reality we all saw unfold. I had seen, even in a small way, what government is willing to do. I had seen how easily power could shift away from protecting people toward controlling them. And I knew what the right side of history would be.

Now, it's not that there are no good people in government institutions, military or otherwise. It's that these systems are set up to punish moral courage and reward institutional loyalty, even when the institution is wrong.

Which brings us to an honorable mention for this chapter, **Col. David Hackworth**. Hackworth was one of the most decorated soldiers in American history. At just fourteen years old, he paid a vagrant to act as his father and sign papers allowing him to join the Merchant Marine. A year later, using those same papers, he enlisted in the United States Army. He would go on to serve with distinction in Korea and Vietnam, eventually earning *seventy-eight* combat decorations and rising to the rank of full Colonel.

I first studied Hackworth while I was a Captain. At that time, I was attending Squadron Officer School—part of the professional military education ladder in the Air Force. One of our assignments was to write a leadership paper. I chose to write about Hackworth and his books *About Face* and *The Vietnam Primer*, which he co-wrote with General S.L.A. Marshall.

My instructors **hated** my paper. They hated that I dared to use someone like Hackworth as a leadership example—a man who had spoken out against his own chain of command, who had criticized the way the Vietnam War was run, and who had done so while he was a full-bird Colonel, selected for War College and on track to become a General.

But that's exactly why Hackworth mattered—and why he still matters today. He made a conscious decision to speak out when it cost him everything. He knew what it would cost him; it would end his career. But he did it anyway—because it was the right thing to do.

That's moral courage. That's being *great* by being *good*. By knowingly, willingly sacrificing your success, your ambition, and your own good name in order to protect others. That's something very special. It's Hackworth's way. Washington's, before anyone. Jefferson Davis's and Winston Churchill's way. It's the American way.

The clarity of moral courage reveals what to do.

Every single time.

Now . . . will **you** do it?

Who You Must Become to Do Something About It

By now, you understand what it takes to act. You've learned how to channel your pain, your anger, and your conviction into real-world movement. You've also learned how real victories can be won. Waiting for someone else to fix it is not the American way. And so we come to understand the system well enough to beat it at its own game. Then now in Part II, we will turn inwards, from the mission to the one leading it: you.

Here, abstract becomes concrete. Strategy becomes execution. Stop being a frustrated observer; become a cultural insurgent. Part II builds directly on what you learned in Part I, especially the idea that we don't win by appeasing the Left's institutions or by begging for permission from any given system they control. We win by building new systems. Parallel systems. Local systems.

Real-life alternatives to the fake options they've given us. This is what *we* do.

So in Part II, you'll see how Americans like you—ordinary citizens with extraordinary commitment—are already doing this. They're showing up at school board meetings not (just) to shout but win. They're launching media platforms, businesses, and ministries from which speak truth without fear, or rather . . . in spite of all fear. They're running for office; the office is running for them.

Now understand this: Once you step up, you *will* be targeted. The machine will come for you. Not always through direct attacks but through slander, isolation, financial pressure, and public humiliation attempts. In Part II, you'll learn exactly how to handle it. From navigating media hit pieces to surviving betrayal from your own side, you'll get real-world examples, strategies, and hard-earned wisdom from someone who's lived it—and refused to back down.

You'll also learn how to keep going even when the easy thing is to quit. Even when the people who should support you stay silent. Even when doing the right thing means being hated by the wrong people. Because that's what it means to be part of a real movement.

Part II is your guide to taking ground and holding it. It's about knowing the terrain, anticipating the attacks, and building communities that are stronger than the cancel mobs, more resilient than political operatives, and more faithful than the institutions that betrayed us.

This is where you become un-cancellable. You will not hide who you really are; you will reveal who you really are.

Let's get to work. The future won't wait.

CHAPTER 7

Why You Would Fail (And How Not To)

Do you know how Barack Obama became president? From obscurity as a far-left organizer, to ultimately a far-left presidential administration—how did he do it? Well, before becoming President, Obama started his political career in corrupt Chicago, where he worked as a community organizer. He later became an activist-attorney and radically progressive academic, teaching at the University of Chicago Law School. He then transitioned to a political career, serving as an Illinois State Senator from 1997 to 2004. Following that, he won a seat in the U.S. Senate in 2004, representing Illinois, before running for president in 2008. So what opened the door for him to enter national politics, first as a federal senator? Failure. But not his.

Have you heard of Jack Ryan? No, not Tom Clancy's Jack Ryan—Obama's Jack Ryan. Barack Obama's expected opponent in the 2004 U.S. Senate race, Republican Jack Ryan, withdrew in

June after scandalous divorce records were unsealed, revealing allegations that he (again, allegedly) tried to pressure his ex-wife, actress Jeri Ryan, into "public sex acts." Specifically:

> *It was revealed that six years earlier, Jeri accused Jack of asking her to perform sexual acts with him in public and in sex clubs in New York, New Orleans and Paris. Jeri described one venue as "a bizarre club with cages, whips, and other apparatus hanging from the ceiling." Jack denied the allegations. Although Jeri only made a brief statement, and refused to comment on the matter during the campaign, the disclosure led Jack to withdraw his candidacy[8].*

In August, with under three months to Election Day, the Illinois GOP tapped Alan Keyes—a Maryland resident who then established legal residency in Illinois—to replace him.

Obama and Keyes sparred in three televised debates, disagreeing on abortion, gun rights, school choice, tax cuts, and stem cell research, among other things. Keyes and others criticized Obama's record of "present" votes on abortion-related bills. Everything about the campaign from then on was catastrophic for Republicans; Obama won the general election in a landslide, taking 70 percent of the vote to Keyes's 27 percent—the largest margin in Illinois history—flipping 92 of 102 counties. The collapse of Ryan's campaign ultimately cut for Obama a clean, clear path to national attention and true political power.

Now, consider Ryan's defense at the time. He said on television:

> *[This] is the first sexless sex scandal because there was no sex, and the person involved was my wife, so I don't think it's really a matter of relevance for the political campaign and said that since the documents were released by the judge in California[9].*

---

8   John Chase and Liam Ford, "Ryan File a Bombshell," *Chicago Tribune*, June 22, 2004, http://www.chicagotribune.com/2004/06/22/ryan-file-a-bombshell/

9   "Jack Ryan on Sex Scandal and Dropping Out of Senate Race," *NBC News*, June 25, 2004, http://www.nbcnews.com/id/wbna5386298.

But it was too late. Not for us. Ryan's example reveals how important it is to reign in our appetites and clamp down on our flaws—and neutralize our own potential for unforced errors. The most far-left, anti-American administration, which permanently brought "woke" politics into the culture, came about in large part because Jack Ryan's scandal and subsequent shame paved the way.

Now, I'm not going to condemn Jack Ryan personally. The reason any good man or woman may fail in our objective to do something of significance to better our country is usually of our own doing. "We're our own worst enemy," the saying goes. Here's what we can do about that.

HOW TO FIGHT YOURSELF (AND WIN)

It's how you learn to perform despite your flaws and weaknesses—and how you deal with failure—that ultimately enables increased ability and, in my opinion, winning outcomes.

First let's talk about **temper**. Boy, do I have one. Growing up, I was a sickly little guy and often couldn't keep up with my older brothers. One way I compensated was by getting mad at myself—so mad that I'd generate the energy or strength to push through whatever we were doing. It didn't always work, but it worked enough for me to feel good about it. Unfortunately, in doing so, I developed a wicked temper. That anger, while usually directed inward, would sometimes leak out and get aimed at others—even today. I try hard to guard against it, but when it does happen, it always catches me—and whoever it's aimed at—completely by surprise. Because as you can probably tell from my voice, most of the time I'm the level-headed, strategic thinker in the room.

Obviously, popping off—especially when you're a military commander—doesn't usually lead to success, unless you're doing it deliberately for a specific reason. It's also not a healthy trait to have as a husband and a dad. It disrupts the trust and love that your family needs from you at every moment.

When I was commanding a B-1 bomber squadron during my last combat deployment in 2005, there was an incident with my temper that I still lose sleep over. One of my officers, a young captain, had a career trajectory similar to my own—but with even more remarkable experience. I saw him as a hero. Before he became a pilot and our squadron life support officer, he had served as an air liaison officer with the Army Rangers. He had jumped into Afghanistan on the first night of the Global War on Terror after 9/11 and earned a gold combat star for his wings. That kind of experience is rare in the Air Force. I had a lot of respect for him and tried to mentor him, giving him leadership opportunities to help him advance toward command.

But during the maximum effort mission I described earlier—targeting a high-value enemy—I lost my temper. I was completely exhausted. The issue was small, almost laughable. In the cold desert winter, he had done his job and gotten cold-weather gear for the aircrews after we'd transitioned from flying in the tropics. Everyone had warm jackets—except me. And instead of appreciating that he was being selfless by making sure everyone else was taken care of first, I snapped. I yelled at him for not putting me first, which was totally selfish. I was getting ready to fly. It was cold. I lost it. He was stunned. He took his jacket off and gave it to me. And I took it—from someone I deeply admired. I permanently damaged that relationship at that moment.

There were consequences. Word got out, and while we completed the deployment successfully, that one outburst had ripple effects I had to work hard to overcome—some I never did. That officer ended up arrested for DUI not long after we got home. I got a call in the middle of the night from a local cop—a Gulf War vet—who told me the officer had even called him a terrorist. I told the officer to go ahead and book him for the night.

The next day, my ops officer and I showed up in dress blues

to bail him out. That's when I realized the full extent of the harm I'd done. Instead of being humbled, the officer yelled at me right there in the police station. My ops officer asked me to leave the room, gave the man a proper dressing down, and we got him out. But I was still the commander—and I had to take action under military law. I was forced to discipline him, and his once-promising career was knocked off the command track.

I may have done that to myself, too, by the way. During my State House race, I was hosting my first radio show on 990 AM out of New Orleans. I kept hosting the show even while I was campaigning for state legislature, and honestly, I should've won that race. I had the support to do it. (But if you Google "Rob Maness" and "blow me," you'll find the story that probably did some damage—though I can't say exactly how much.)

Now, I never apologized for that incident. I'm a military guy; I've served both as an enlisted man and an officer. I talk rough sometimes—and I'm not sorry about it. I might give a heads-up at the beginning of a talk, especially if I've got a room full of Republican women, and say, "Hey, just so you know, you might hear some words you're not used to hearing." I try not to cuss, but it slips out every now and then.

At the time, I was listening to talk radio guys like Mark Levin and Michael Savage for style. One thing they did that I picked up on was how they handled troll callers—they'd cut them off, yell at them, use strong language. So one night, this guy who went by "The Flaming Liberal," a regular caller, phones in. I think my opponents put him up to it. He called me an extremist, and I went off on him. He started swearing at me too. In the middle of all that, I said, "Blow me." That was it. No profanity. Just, "Blow me." Then I cut him off.

Well, the next day I got a call from a reporter I knew—she was actually a friend.

She said, "Sir, I really don't want to do this story, but I have to. CBS is doing a hit piece on you."

Turns out, the network had bleeped the audio to make it sound like I'd dropped the f-bomb, even though I didn't use a single actual swear word. The guy had been swearing at me, and they bleeped both of us. I wasn't having it.

So I called the producer and said, "You'd better release the full audio or put up a transcript, because I didn't cuss once—and if you don't fix it, I'll sue."

He pushed back and said, "Well, you said 'blow me.' Is that what a little girl should hear on the radio?"

I told him, "First of all, the show airs at nine at night. If a six-year-old girl is up listening to AM radio at that hour, we've got bigger issues—like who's parenting her."

Eventually, they made some edits and left the clip up, but I'm thankful that reporter called me. I later wrote an op-ed, and I still haven't apologized. Because I won't. I'll come back to that in a little bit.

We may not all have statehouse races to worry about, but we all nonetheless have our **vices** to battle. Smoking cigarettes, drinking alcohol, and partying were just part of life as a young man—especially in the military. EOD troops and military aviators are some of the hardest-partying cultures in the US armed forces, and yes, we lived up to that reputation! Fortunately, I was smart enough to quit smoking in my thirties and learn to moderate my drinking. Because of that, now in my sixties, I'm in good health and I had a successful career to show for it. Not everyone is so fortunate or wise, as the DUI bit earlier illustrates . . .

And then of course there are just our own personal **failures** that we have to overcome, mitigate, or otherwise prevent, if at all possible. I've had many failures—but how we deal with failure is what ultimately creates success, if we handle it well.

I failed out of pilot training. That broke my heart. Ever since I could walk, I wanted to be a fighter pilot, having grown up in an Air Force family. So what did I do? I didn't quit. I sought out other flying opportunities in the Air Force and won a slot in navigator training. That launched a highly successful career that led to me being selected for command three times—something only two to three percent of all Air Force officers ever achieve.

Personally, I also failed in my first marriage. I was only nineteen when my first son was born. We just didn't have the experience or maturity to stick with it—especially me. I consider that my greatest leadership failure. As a husband, I was supposed to lead and hold the marriage together, but my youth and inexperience blinded me to the ways I was failing my wife and kids until it was too late.

Thankfully, my ex-wife and I were still able to work together, and I stayed focused on my son and daughter from that marriage. Today, I'm blessed by their successes—and by some fantastic grandsons—because I was able to work hard and change course as a father, and later, as a husband in my second marriage.

God has been my rock through every struggle—mine and my family's. His forgiveness for my many flaws and transgressions is the foundation that keeps me steady now.

NO MATTER WHAT, NEVER DO THIS

Now, regardless of which you may be most concerned about—temper, vices, or outright failures—I will give you this golden advice: **Never apologize to the mob.** What matters most is not what happens before a controversy, but how you respond when it happens and after it happens. That's when true leadership is tested. Good leaders are self-aware, yes—but awareness isn't the same as weakness.

Fix yourself before the fight, as best you can, knowing you will not be perfect, while also deciding ahead of time that you will feel no shame or utter no "sorry," lest you give up and surrender your proverbial US senate seat to a radical anti-Americanist.

Consider also that some failures are successes in disguise, or can be. For some, a moderated vice—when properly understood and channeled—can become a tool. My temper, for example, is a tool. It can be destructive if unchecked, but when properly focused, it becomes an asset in leadership, especially under fire. And think about President Trump. His utterly frank New York personality, his bluntness—what many consider a vice—actually resonates. He says what others won't say but what 50 percent of the public is already thinking, word for word. Some say it's crass; I say it's correct.

Now, you may be able to transmute vice into value, but there is probably one great weakness you cannot overcome. I could not. You may have no choice in the matter. I owe it to you to tell you about it so you can mentally and emotionally prepare yourself for it: Our worst failing may not be our own. It's **betrayal**.

THE WORST WEAKNESS: NOT EVEN YOURS

Treachery can neither be mitigated or prevented. But it can be expected. And when it's expected, or at least anticipated as coming with the territory, you will not be too trusting. You will keep your secrets close; this, I believe, is one way we can be "wise as serpents and innocent as doves," as the Bible says.

Do I have a betrayal story for you. But first, some background. Let me go back to my 2014 Senate race—before Trump ran. The big three policies we were pushing were border security, ending endless wars, and energy independence. Sound familiar? Trump's top three ended up being basically the same. I didn't know who he was back then—I'd never even heard of the guy's political positions, really—but looking back, it's clear we were tapping into the same zeitgeist.

That's the word—zeitgeist. We had it. We raised $3.5 million for a guy not born in Louisiana, fresh out of the military after 30 years, and who had never run for office. Not bad. And while I was still a political neophyte and naive about a lot, I was a solid candidate with a message that caught fire.

The one thing I didn't have yet was that next-level communication talent. I could speak plainly. I could connect. I had the courage to tell the truth as I saw it, no matter the blowback. But I wasn't a television communicator. Not yet. And that's the missing piece Trump had from day one.

Trump doesn't just communicate—he performs. It's acting, in a way, but also something more. He says the things people are thinking but are too afraid to say out loud. That's a rare gift. And even now, he's getting sharper. He's mastering the craft. Whatever you call it—storytelling, raw honesty, dramatic timing—it works.

Back in 2016, I was a Ted Cruz guy during the primaries. But let's be honest—Cruz wasn't who he claimed to be. He wasn't the outsider, the Tea Party rebel, the truth-teller he portrayed. When he dropped out, it was clear to me: Trump was the only one who could actually pull this off.

That year, while Trump was making headlines, I was running again for US senate. My campaign manager was Andy Surabian— Andy is a great guy. An Armenian powerhouse. He's the one who introduced me to the word "zeitgeist." After my campaign, Andy went to work in Trump Tower, ended up being Bannon's strategy aide in the White House, and now works with Don, Jr. He helped run JD Vance's campaign and supported Bernie Moreno, too—same as I did. Andy's still running the Save America PAC for Don, Jr. Anyway, somehow, we got him into the Trump war room. And I'll tell you something: Trump tells this story about the phrase "drain the swamp"—how someone whispered it to him and told him to start saying it. Well, Sarah Palin had recorded a radio ad for my campaign where that exact phrase was used. Andy knew that. So I'm pretty sure it was Andy who whispered that to

Trump. I've never gotten to sit down with him long enough to ask, but that's my hypothesis—because not long after that, *boom*, it was everywhere.

Back in the 2016 Louisiana floods, Hillary and Obama wouldn't come. So we called Trump's team through Andy and said, "Get him down here." My campaign manager at the time acted as the advance man. He got Trump into a briefing with the sheriff and emergency ops center, and took him to visit flood victims. Great media moment. That's when his campaign really started to catch momentum.

Rewind now. Back to 2014, when my Senate campaign was peaking. We'd raised over a million dollars. Sarah Palin was coming in for the Southern Republican Leadership Conference in New Orleans. We got her to do a rally with us the night before. The room was packed—standing room only, shoulder to shoulder. I don't know how we didn't get booted for a fire code violation. There's video; it was electric. We were within six points of knocking Bill Cassidy out of the jungle primary and going head-to-head with Mary Landrieu. Head-to-head, we were polling at 53 percent. But raw polling data in a jungle primary doesn't always tell the full story—it showed me at about 8 percent, so people underestimated us.

Anyway, I was scheduled to go on the FOX News personality Sean Hannity's show that night with Sarah Palin. That coverage likely would have clinched the race for me. But right before it was time, I got pulled back—"You've been canceled." They replaced me with Cassidy, didn't tell Palin, and blindsided both of us. That's when I knew the GOP establishment was pulling strings to make sure Cassidy won. Hannity . . . well, I'll just say this: My opinion of him has only gone down since.

The next day, we hear Trump's coming to speak at the conference. My strategist Jason Recher—a great, trustworthy guy—gets me a meeting with Trump through an advance team member. We go back to the green room, and I walk halfway across the room toward Trump.

"Mr. Trump, this is Colonel Maness, running for Senate."

Trump doesn't even let him finish. He waves a paper at me—polling data—and says, "You're only at eight percent. Get outta here."

I didn't argue. I said, "Nice to meet you," and left. Jason couldn't believe it. Fifteen minutes later, I got a call. "Come back. They want to try again."

I said, "Are you sure?" But I went. Same room. Walk in again. Trump looks up from his speech notes and says, "I already told you—you can't get it done. Get outta here." That was it. I turned around and left again.

It turns out, Scott McKay of The Hayride—a GOP establishment outlet in Louisiana—was in the room and wrote a hit piece about me. It was embarrassing. Trump had actually called me out by name during his speech and told me to drop out. Then he did it *again* in a press conference after. Clearly, Republican leadership wanted Cassidy and were using Trump to make it happen.

I was angry. Really angry. It felt disrespectful. But the best advice I got came from Jason afterward. He closed the door, kicked everyone out of the room, and said. "Rob, never talk about this in public. Ever."

And I didn't. Not for ten years. I've acknowledged the story but never told it—until now. Jason was right. Trump was a unique individual. And I'm proud to say I kept my mouth shut. Because in the end, I'm proud that Donald J. Trump is the 47th president of the United States. I've forgiven much. It certainly helps that when JD Vance announced his US senate run in Ohio, I was one of the first to endorse him as the Republican candidate. I urged Donald Trump to endorse JD, he did, and the rest is history. I've forgiven much.

Just not Hannity.

What You Can Do About It

CHAPTER 8

What You Are Missing (And How to Find It)

It takes a lot of things to be a person in public life who leads organizations in positions like military commander or elected official. One common trait I did not possess is **extroversion**. Public life demands a great deal of energy, and much of that energy goes into projecting an outgoing personality—especially if you're not naturally wired that way.

I'm an introvert by nature. Dealing with hundreds or even thousands of people regularly is physically and mentally exhausting for me. I had to teach myself how to be an extrovert. I succeeded— and if you had asked my wife Candy early in our marriage how she manages being married to an introvert, she would have given you a strange look and said something like, "What are you talking about? I can't get Rob to stop talking with people when we go into a room." At least, that's what she used to say until I explained to her that I really am an introvert. That helped her understand why I hide in my office after an event or don't want to talk right away—because being around people drains me completely, and I need solitude to recharge.

My point is this: We can train and educate ourselves to overcome even the most naturally ingrained limitations and develop the traits needed for success. It's not easy, and it takes a long time—but it can be done. I've now given speeches to audiences of thousands, something I never imagined myself doing as a young man. In fact, almost every day I speak to thousands and interact with a live audience that averages well over a thousand people. I also thrive in one-on-one conversations and town hall settings where I can answer questions directly from people I've never met.

A second trait I'll highlight here because I would not be here without it is **endurance**. Human beings are capable of achieving incredible mental and physical outcomes, even with little or no formal training. We're naturally built to push beyond what we think is possible. Some of us may be naturally good at things like running long distances, but to consistently finish an endurance race like a competitive marathon requires dedicated training—of both mind and body.

My main profession, of course, is the military, and in our world—whether on the ground, in the air, or at sea—endurance is often the essential trait. While we don't train people to run marathons, we do train them to endure feats like flying thirty-six-hour combat missions, or completing a night combat jump into enemy territory and navigating terrain at 10,000 feet elevation with minimal support. Endurance also looks like volunteering in a crisis, as hundreds of us did on 9/11 at the Pentagon. We went back in to find survivors and fight the fire all day. Even though it wasn't something we were trained for specifically, we were so well-prepared overall that we spent the entire day breathing smoke and jet fuel fumes without giving the time a second thought—until we were finally ordered out as the sun was setting. "Time flies" isn't a cliché; it's real when you're engaged in a mission of endurance and mentally prepared for any outcome.

Endurance also shows up in unexpected ways. During my first US Senate race in 2013 and into 2014 against Mary Landrieu and Bill Cassidy in Louisiana, my trusted friend, personal security man, and driver, Neal "Chip" Wood, and I spent eighteen months driving my Ford F-150 more than 87,000 miles—covering every parish in the state three times. That was its own endurance test, but it came close to being a winning strategy. Unfortunately, it was derailed by forces we couldn't anticipate—one of them named Donald J. Trump, whose story weaved its way into mine in the last chapter. But the effort launched my entrance into the political arena, where I still stand today after many battles and victories, including Donald Trump's successful re-election in 2024.

Without extroversion and endurance, I would not be here; this book would not be here. There would be no story of trials and triumphs to tell. Just the trials. Nobody would want to read that. There would be nothing to learn from that.

This is the key insight I want to impart to you through this chapter: Where you're going, you're going to need personality traits, skill sets, and inner strengths that you likely don't yet have. *And you don't even know what they are yet.* See, I didn't even know what I was missing in my career—until it happened. Self-awareness didn't come easy. Life came hard. To win the game, I had to learn the rules; I had to wield two special tools: extroversion and endurance.

You may need these as well. But I have a hunch there will be other traits you need along your way. People who go up against Left-wing, anti-American strongholds have it tough—and if you're reading this, it's because that fight is yours, too. You'll need the right repertoire to succeed in the battles ahead. The era of polite debate is over. This is closer to warfare now—and politics, after all, has always been warfare by other means.

ESSENTIAL TRAITS TO WIN (THAT MOST PEOPLE LACK)

What traits do you need that you don't have? Most people need (and don't have) **thick skin**. Here's what I mean by that.

THICK SKIN (TO OUTLAST AND WIN)

One of the essential traits needed to win in today's world is **thick skin**—real thick skin. And I don't just mean being able to take a joke or brush off someone saying something mean. I'm talking about enduring a coordinated campaign—journalists, activists, lawyers, social media influencers, even elected officials—all well-funded and well-connected, doing everything they can to psychologically destroy you. Not just smear your name. Not just cost you your job. Their end goal is to drive you to suicide. That's what happens to those on the side of right who are effective. Not all of us—but the ones who pose a real threat. That's the level of psychological warfare we're dealing with.

It's happened before. Some of the January 6th political prisoners were driven to that point. It's not new either—go back to the Soviet gulags. One of the tactics used to keep costs down was pushing prisoners to take their own lives. The idea was to break a person so thoroughly that they lost all hope—and then everyone around them abandoned them. As Jack Posobiec and Joshua Lisec write in *Unhumans* about far-left-wing movements throughout history, "This is what they do."

Your skin better be like bronzed leather—like *armor*. Because these people aren't just trying to disagree with you.

They're trying to eliminate you. And they're relentless. That's why it's so important to never apologize to the mob. *Ever.* Even if you think maybe you said something the wrong way—or that, back in the day, you might've handled it differently. You can't give the Left an inch. Because they're already charging the gates, making things up if they have to, looking for cracks to exploit. One apology opens the floodgates.

There's this whole interconnected web—across professions, politics, media, academia—all unified by one thing: a belief in some form of totalitarianism. That's really the best word for it. Total control. Doesn't matter if it's called Marxism, progressivism, collectivism, technocracy—it's all the same beast. And that entire machine exists to destroy individuals who threaten their grip on power. It still surprises me sometimes that this is happening in America. I shouldn't be surprised anymore, but I still am.

They don't want to win the debate; they want to eliminate the debate. They know their ideas can't win. So instead of winning on merit, they destroy anyone who stands in their way. They use force, manipulation, coercion—anything except open, honest persuasion. That's the game now. The promise of equality is a lie; the only way to fulfill that promise is to make everyone equally poor, weak, ugly, and miserable. That's how you level things—by cutting down anyone who dares to rise above. "This is what they do."

If you dare to push back, they don't just want to silence you; they want to erase you. That's why you have to be unbreakable. And unapologetic. Grow some skin. It better be thick.

A SENSE OF HUMOR (TO SEND THEM PACKING)

A **sense of humor** might be one of the most underrated psychological weapons you can have—not just about yourself, but about the enemy, too. *If you can't laugh at them, they win.* But if you can't laugh at yourself, no one will want to **follow** you.

I deploy humor all the time (now that I'm an extrovert), especially when I give speeches. Just last night, as of this very writing I was speaking at a County Republican Executive Committee meeting. I made sure to add in some self-deprecating humor, especially about my own mistakes or moments where I didn't perform at my best (several of which you've already read about in this very book). Because if people can't see you laugh at yourself, they're not going to give you their trust, their money, or their vote. You just may need all three.

And when it comes to our opponents, mockery breaks them. In their book, Jack and Joshua call it "The Unhuman's Bane." Laughter disarms them completely. They don't know what to do with ridicule. They've been trained to wield outrage like a weapon, so when someone smirks or cracks a joke at their expense, their nervous system malfunctions. They expect fear and deference. What they can't handle is laughter. They break; they glitch. Some of them . . . run.

Understand that we're not being "mean." The Left is unhinged. The performative nature of their rage, their public meltdowns . . . it's absurd, which is the point. And see, when you frame it as Left-wing performance art, it becomes almost entertaining. You film it. You mock it. You make a meme out of it. ***You turn it into a joke, because it is a joke.*** Because that's what they are. A spectacle. A parody of themselves.

Don't meet their fury with more fury. Meet it with mockery. Use satire. Memes. Laughter. Turn them into the joke they already are. It's nothing new. Back in pre-communications technology history, we used effigies for the same purpose: political satire, visual mockery. It's always been one of the most effective ways to knock down tyrants and expose absurd ideologies for what they really are. So learn to take a joke, but just as importantly, learn to give them. Give them so good they can't take it. Make them pack up their stuff and go home.

EDGE THINKING (THAT PIERCES THE OVERTON WINDOW)

Another essential quality is what I call "**edge thinking**." It's not (just) about being "edgy" or provocative for the sake of social media engagement or whatever other goal you might have. Edge thinking, specifically when done out loud, strategically pushes the boundaries of acceptable conversation, shifting the Overton Window. It's having the guts and imagination to reframe public perception around a topic, inserting new, sharper angles into discourse in ways that seem almost . . . casual. This might be more than shifting the Overton Window; it's throwing knives through it, metaphorically speaking.

- One example of this is, going back to Jack and Joshua and their book *Unhumans*, came when Joshua gave interviews about cultural Marxist infiltration of local libraries and schools. He called out various pro-homosexuality picture books (yes, picture books!) that depicted graphic sexual acts between, among other things, gay men—and again, the audience is for children. Liberal librarians happily give this reading material to children ("This is what they do."). And so when Joshua brought this up, and he mentioned this propaganda, he referred to it as, "LGTBQMAP." We all know the first part of that acronym; few know the latter part. "MAP" stands for "Minor-Attracted Persons." You know what that means. So does Joshua, which is why he deliberately ties the two identity groups together. Personally, I have no quarrel with various gay Republicans I've known and worked with; I pray for their salvation as I do every soul who crosses my path in some meaningful way. My point now is Joshua's edge thinking: to plant associations others don't want you to make, but to do it in such a way that you can't easily be dismissed as outrageous or unserious. It truly is exploitative of children to thrust upon them pornographic material in the name of "gay history" or "LGBT rights" or "queer theory" and whatever else the paper-flimsy excuse is. As Joshua says, once again, "This is what they do."

What we all must do in our various Americanist journeys is to push that Overton Window of acceptable discourse open in the other direction. You know you're engaging in real edge thinking when people on your own side say, "Wait—you can do that?" Jack and Joshua did this in *Unhumans*, for example, by bringing forward historical figures like Francisco Franco and Augusto Pinochet—not in the typical way they're discussed, but by highlighting the **positive** aspects of their governance. That's not just outside the Overton Window. That's outside the house the window belongs to. So they just knocked the whole damn wall out.

Now, the key with edge thinking in public is *sincerity*. It has to be delivered as if everyone already knows it's true. No dramatic mic-drop moment. No signaling that what you're saying is provocative. It has to come off as obvious, natural, and shared in belief by all who listen. That way it slips through the defenses more effectively—you're not triggering the usual neurological alarm system people have for "controversial ideas."

The goal is to expand the public's frame of acceptable thought to include all the things you believe but aren't supposed to say. The Left has already done this; they've defined the bounds of polite discourse. That's why their political language is always about being "nonpartisan" or "reaching across the aisle." What they really mean is, "We want Republicans to agree with us." And conservatives have fallen for it for years. They get rewarded with TV spots on MSNBC for parroting Left-approved soundbites. "This is what they do."

Not anymore.

NONCONFORMITY (WHEN THERE'S NO ONE TO DEFEND YOURS)

Have you ever seen that image of that one guy in the sea of people refusing to do the Hitler salute—arms all up, except for him, circled in red? He was the wrench in the German war machine's gears. Sometimes people call a man such as this a "voice in the wilderness." It's the one who is willing to stand alone, even to be exiled. Or worse. **Nonconformity** captures that stubborn refusal to bow, even when no one will defend you. It's closely tied to moral courage—but not just such courage in theory. It's the practiced, lived-out version that doesn't back down when things get (too) personal or lonely. It's having the guts to stand alone without flinching.

Right-wing organizers like Jack Posobiec and Mike Cernovich have it. They're willing to be lied about, to be insulted by their own side, to be made fun of by other people in their movement to their faces—and laugh it all off afterwards. They say the unsayable, get edgy, and don't flinch when they're the only ones doing it. Well, one woman I know like them is Cassandra MacDonald. She's probably the best example of a modern-day, Right-wing woman who consistently shows this same courageous nonconformity. Years ago, she was reporting on Julian Assange before it was "safe" or popular to do so, and she called out the federal government without hesitation. That's when I first started following her. Cassandra's sharp and well-informed, and she doesn't just fire off hot takes without reading the research. That's a big difference from Jane-come-latelys, who skim the surface and don't double-check their facts—and a story they thought was real turns out to be fake, and the blowup is a colossal embarrassment to the entire Republican party. As President Trump might say, "Many such cases."

Cassandra's different—more deliberate, more principled. And since she became a mother of twins, she's stepped back a bit from the spotlight. That's understandable. Motherhood changes things. It softens. But fatherhood? Fatherhood makes a man more based—more aggressive. More willing to fight. Like Cerno and Poso. People misunderstand them constantly, even when they use plain language. That's just how far ahead they think. I expect it's lonely over there. I also expect it's worth it.

Which brings me to the final sobering point of this chapter, of which there have been many. You know that old saying, "History is written by the victors"? In our case—should we win—our history will be written by sore losers, no matter what. Just look at the Wikipedia pages of people like Jack or Mike. Or maybe don't. Every salacious rumor, every false claim, every exaggerated quote taken out of context—everything that can be compiled against you, will be. That's the reality.

Some of us don't even get a page at all. It's been tried, but Wikipedia won't allow it. What matters is the willingness—and ability—to endure a relentless smear campaign. To stand tall, even when your skin has to be thick as armor. To keep a sense of humor, even when you're face-to-face with someone who could very well get physically violent. To think creatively—edgily— about how to push the conversation forward. And most of all, to be the one who dares when no one else will. The nonconformist. The single voice. The last one standing. Because even if you win, even if you succeed on the issue that matters most, your enemies will write the story. So the only question that remains is: Are you still willing to do it?

I am. The ultrawinning football coach Vince Lombardi had a quote which now comes to mind:

Winning isn't everything; it's the only thing.

If we don't win—if **you** don't win—then all is lost. "Doom and gloom, Rob, wow." Yes, that's correct. Understand something: The number-one priority of the Left is *power*. After that, they put into practice their principles, such as envy and resentment. That's what guides them. But power is what *empowers* them. They seek first authority, then everything else. We the people must do the same. Power first, then principles. And I don't mean Senator Mitch McConnell-style power, where you're hanging on to your job no matter what it costs the country. I mean *will*. The *will* to make things happen, and the *will* to follow through until your enemies fall in line. This is your charge. Please accept it. Power, then principles like righteousness, justice, charity, and so on. But put principles before power, and you'll have neither.

It will be a lonely road. But you will not be alone for long. Those who went before you will call you up. And that's what our very next chapter is about. Let's go up.

CHAPTER 9

The Resources You'll Need (And How to Attract Them)

Here's a secret many people miss about military command: It's not about you as the commander; it's always about the mission given to you by the American people and the team you're leading. Unfortunately, the system we put officers through to develop them for command opportunities specifically drives them to focus on themselves and their own development before their subordinates. It's strange, isn't it? Every professional military institution teaches you to be selfless, to put others before yourself. But at the same time, it makes clear that if you don't focus on your own career, you'll never be a commander.

Those who recognize this conflict of interest and learn how to deal with it effectively are successful. As for those who don't? Well, the trail of tears to command is littered with their carcasses—and those should be used as valuable lessons for those who follow.

So the question is: How do you succeed in highly competitive fields, whether it's the military, politics, or the business world? Or for our purposes, on the battlefield of culture and society where winners take all? First, the people you come into contact with along the trail—no matter their status—are extremely important, even if you're starting out as an E-1 in the Air Force like I did. Each of them, whether peer or superior, becomes part of your life network. And if you figure this out early (I didn't), the more successful you'll be in any endeavor.

Over time, staying in touch with them is critically important—and difficult to do—especially in a fast-moving environment like the military, where you move every two years or so. The point is: It's about the right people.

I've mentioned many of my core network team members so far in this book. Among that group, having mentors with more experience than you is also very important. Without my mentors and friends like (now) Brigadier General Jonathan George, Colonel Jack Wiley, Colonel Bill Moran, Lt. General Bob Elder, Lt. General Ron Henderson, Brigadier General Jim "Rev" Jones, Senior Master Sergeant Jim Powlas, Chief Master Sergeant Tommy Randolph, Master Sergeant Junior Ladd, and Marine Lt. Benjamin O. Bell, I would never have become an EOD man, an officer, a combat aviator, a B-1 Squadron Commander of the oldest bomber squadron in the Air Force, Vice Commander of America's only airborne intelligence wing, or Commander of the sixth-largest strategic installation in the world. I would never have attended Harvard's John F. Kennedy School of Government or the US Naval War College, long considered the "Harvard" of American war colleges. And without mentors like Governor Sarah Palin and Jason Recher, I wouldn't have had even the modest success in politics that I've achieved.

Of course, I've used the word "I" in all of this, but it really should be "we." This life of leadership is a team thing, not an individual thing, and I owe them everything.

That leads me to the next thing you'll need, besides people (and we'll return shortly to how **you** can find your own people). You're going to need money. Funding. Especially if you're stepping into the political arena or any domain parallel to it.

Learning how to raise capital is one of the most difficult tasks I've ever taken on. In politics, it's thankless. And when you're an outsider who's not a billionaire, every donor you call invariably says you can't possibly win—because you're opposing the party and its leadership.

People like Senator Mitch McConnell have already called them and told them to give only to his political action committee— and he will sort out what candidates deserve support. Yes, I know that sounds crazy, but it's true; the owner of an NFL team told me that directly.

For those outside the establishment, the next resource you need is the support of average people—what we call "the base" or "grassroots" in politics   in very large numbers, to make up for the money you won't be able to raise.

I've already mentioned a few of the folks who helped build my grassroots network that covered the entire state of Louisiana, people like Robbye St. Pierre, Kelly Camp, Mary Kass. And I'll add one more here: Krista Carter from West Monroe, Louisiana, who not only helped me with fundraising, but also built out our network in northern Louisiana. That happened after Jason Recher and Governor Palin were able to get me meetings with some folks named Phil and Alan Robertson, the Duck Commanders. I've always said from that first Senate campaign that we didn't need as much money as the establishment candidates, who both spent over $15 million. We just needed enough to whoop them.

Circling back to networks and mentoring—the other "human

resource" you need, and need to be actively building, is the network of those who will come after you. In the military, command jobs only last eighteen months to two years. So always mentoring your replacements is a constant process. Some of the men and women I mentored in the Air Force have gone on to become generals and wing commanders after their own squadron commands. The same applies in politics. That's why I've supported JD Vance and, more recently, Bernie Moreno for US Senate. They're my versions of growing the network of those who will come after me. And of course, we now know the most successful of them all, President Donald J. Trump.

Now, this all sounds well and swell. But how do you actually *do* it? Attract the mentors, sponsors, and successors? How do you build a coalition to fulfill your vision? Well, in general, especially when it comes to matters of great cultural significance (and politics is downstream of culture, paraphrasing Andrew Breitbart) . . . the Right has not historically excelled at this.

No man is an island, but conservatives often act like they are. It's time to team up; you'll need every helping hand you can.

Let's zoom out for a bit, for just a moment. By this point in the book, you probably have a sense of what your issue is—what is *the* problem in the broader culture (or in your local area) that you're going to tackle. It's a problem, and now it's your problem, and you are going to solve it, period.

At this point, you should also have a one-sentence statement that describes what you want. Not just what you *don't* want or what you're against, but what you want to create. And it needs to be simple enough that everyone in your charge can understand it, especially those who are under the leadership of your direct reports (whether you have such people now yet or not). Just like in the military, where there are various commanders and then the people under them (and still even more people under *them*), your message needs to be able to filter down clearly to each and every level. Your change-vision should be communicated in a way that your people can repeat it to *their* people.

By now, you also likely also have a sense of the kind of person you need to become over the course of this journey in order to win. I've urged you to think about what could go wrong—what weaknesses or points of potential compromise might create problems for you. And, I hope, you've made the decision: Either you're going to address those weaknesses head-on, or you're going to accept the consequences. Either way, you're never going to apologize. No matter what.

As you stick it out, taking all kinds of flak, you'll realize something: You're not alone. You'll be surrounded by others like you. They're the people who went before, who faced the fire and made it through alive. Those people can become incredible resources. Mentors, possibly. Maybe a sidekick or a full-on partner or two (or more). You might even discover there's already an organization doing the work you were planning to do. In that case, it might be better to join forces, to partner up or affiliate, to confederate in some way, rather than trying to start your own thing from scratch and building a tiny kingdom that's surrounded on all sides by enemy forces and existential threats to progress.

Either way, whether you join up with others or start your own thing, you will need two resources of the mind, which are: **how to organize effectively**, and **how to reward friends and punish enemies**. Now, I want you to re-read that sentence. Think about it . . . Why *these* two? Well, with these two tactical, practical how-to's, the Left has all but conquered our culture, our society, and our very way of life, winning major elections, important lawsuits, and the court of public opinion despite what are otherwise unpopular and unworkable ideas. How much more so will we be able to do good with popular ideas? How much should we?

OK, we'll return to all *that* in a moment, but for now, let's talk organizing among friends.

THE ORGANIZER'S SECRET

A strength the Left has always had is organizing. *Organizing* is pretty much a Left-wing word at this point; it's essentially the entry-level job of all power brokers on the Left. Early in their careers, they were organizers in some way—organizing voters to win a swing district, for example, or organizing against a more moderate Democrat to get a radical candidate elected in a primary. That's the AOC story. It's also Barack Obama's.

Even further back, you find figures like Harvard professor Marshall Ganz, who wrote *People, Power, Change*, colloquially known as "the organizer's handbook." There are entire libraries—both physical and online—of organizing materials and training programs, nearly all of them created by liberals, many of whom are open socialists or even communists.

The Left is effective at self-organization because their tribe has one overarching goal: **power**. Everything else flows from that. They understand the principle of power-first, and then they adopt a certain Leninist framework: the friend/enemy distinction.

THE FRIEND/ENEMY DISTINCTION

First you organize, then you identify friends and enemies. And you reward your friends, and you punish your enemies. There are two sets of standards: one for your friends, and one for your enemies. It's as simple as that.

That's exactly what the old communist revolutionaries would do. For example, if a friend of the Bolshevik cause committed a crime . . . *What crime?* If it was an enemy, it was, *Show me the man, and I'll show you the crime.* That's the Donald J. Trump lawfare situation in a nutshell. They had to twist laws, invent charges, and weaponize regulations. Because he was the enemy. If he had lost the 2024 presidential election, I'm convinced he and his entire family would be spending the rest of their lives in federal prison.

Now, I've brought up power a couple of times, and I want to hammer something home. The Right, particularly conservative, religious people, have traditionally put "principles before power." That's often out of a moral duty, a sense of loyalty to and accountability to God, to something greater than ourselves. But the problem with that becomes rather obvious super-quick. Just take how this shows up in debates over abortion, for example. During the campaign, then-candidate Trump said he's "pro-life," but he also supports exceptions. He didn't say it exactly that way, but the message is clear: In order to govern, you must win. And to win, sometimes, you must message differently than you personally believe. Governing is power. If you don't win, you don't get to govern. And if you don't govern, you can't enact any of your principles. Thus, power comes first. Everything flows from that, whether you're Right or Left. That's something Trump understands deeply, and it's why many 100 percent pro-life people, even those opposed to the death penalty, still support him. He knows how to win. And once you win, you occupy the spaces of power. You act decisively, forcefully. You establish your policy. Then you can talk about principles.

These two guiding ideas—organizing and knowing your friends and enemies—must also be used to build allies. Of course, even the word *ally* has been co-opted by the Left. In practice, on their side, ally means "someone who can do no wrong due to their demographics." For example, if you're an "LGBTQ+ ally," the homosexual or transgender individual in question is automatically right in every dispute. They're defended no matter what. They're given the benefit of the doubt every time. If all of us on the American Right thought the same way and treated everyone allied with us this way, no Democrat would win another election—not even a school board.

THE NEXT QUESTION: *WHO?*

So, who do you want to organize with? These "friends" whom you currently know and soon will?

First, find the people who are already doing what you're doing—people who've suffered through what you're about to go through. Talk to them. Then listen. And see what help they're willing to offer or what opportunities they might have. Again, you might discover, "Actually, we have the perfect role for you," for example. If that role aligns with your single-sentence vision for change, then you can serve *your* cause inside *their* organization. It's easier to run a train on track that's already been laid.

This merits further discussion. A typical conservative trait—which can be a strength but in this context is absolutely a weakness—is rugged individualism. It's the idea that, *I can do everything myself, and therefore I should.* You see this phenomenon both religiously and politically. In American Protestant Christianity, for example, just about anyone can say, "I've been called by God to start a new church. It's my church. I'm the pastor." Even if you have zero members. Congratulations . . . you're now the head of your own church. You're your own pope. You might make it in that regard, or you might not. But if you join an organization that already has thousands—or even millions—of members, you're far more likely to make a bigger difference through that vehicle of existing organization. There's a time and place for individualism, but understand that this is the opposite of organizing. And organizing is what actually holds and wields power. That's what you're going to need if you want to succeed.

The *Unhumans* co-author Joshua Lisec published on X recently this reframe, following the structure originated by persuasion expert and bestselling author Scott Adams in *Reframe Your Brain* (2023):

Usual frame:

Might makes right.

Reframe:

Right needs might.

This is absolutely correct. That reminded me of this sentiment of the Founding Fathers, long-attributed to Benjamin Franklin:

> *We must all hang together, or assuredly we shall all hang separately.*

It's the same idea. There's a time for independent thinking, and there's a time to link arms and work as a team. If you want to *do something*, you organize. It's as simple as that. So, how might it look? Well, team-building might be something as basic as a twenty-minute phone call with someone who's already doing what you want to do, but perhaps for a different cause or on a parallel issue to yours. Their insight might be what helps you pull together a small group of people and make something happen in your own right. Or it might go even further. Maybe they want to partner with you, and now you have a co-founder for a 501(c)(3) or 501(c)(4) nonprofit—or even a for-profit business that serves a higher purpose. There are plenty of for-profit companies started by Americanists who grew tired of cheap Chinese-made crap-products and giant megacorps that promote anti-American values, like DEI or LGBTQ+. If that's your situation, then your organizing might take the form of entrepreneurship. We see this at every conservative, Christian, and right-of-center conference and trade show in America—the various vendor booths are founders and their employees who all got fed up with gay communism and built something better. That's organizing, too.

3 STORIES YOU'LL TELL TO ATTRACT YOUR PEOPLE

Now, you might be wondering how, specifically, you'll be attracting people to your cause—as laborers, volunteers, cofounders, donors, or voters (or all of them). We're going to draw from the organizer extraordinaire himself, Marshall Ganz. He teaches that if you want to organize a movement and take power, you must have three stories, collectively known as the **Public Narrative**:

> *The Public Narrative framework is made up of three components: a Story of Self, a Story of Us, and a Story of Now. A Story of Self communicates the values that have called you to leadership; a Story of Us communicates the values shared by those in action; a Story of Now communicates an urgent challenge to those values that demand action now. Note the quotation from Hillel in the opening to this section: "If I am not for myself, who will be for me? If I am only for myself, what am I? And if not now, when?" (Pirkei Avot Chapter 1:14).*

> *Simply put, Public Narrative says, "Here's who I am, this is what we have in common, and here's what we're going to do about it." By mastering the practise of crafting a narrative that bridges the self, us, and now, organizers enhance their own efficacy and create trust and solidarity with their constituency[10].*

It's intuitive when you read it; it's miraculous when you hear it. When any leader tells their **Story of Self**, **Story of Us**, and **Story of Now** in two minutes or less, even in thirty seconds or less, everyone within earshot gets goosebumps. *Whoa . . . this person is going places . . . and I must go with them.* Every changemaker in history has told such a compelling Public Narrative, including

---

10   Leading Change Network et al., "The Power of Story: The Story of Self, Us and Now," *The Commons Social Change Library*, accessed April 21, 2026, https://commonslibrary. org/the-power-of-story-the-story-of-self-us-and-now/.

the best example of all: Jesus Christ.

To put them all another way, the Story of Self is how your life ties to the cause you're committed to. Can you help people see why this matters to you? And the Story of Us is how "we"—that is, the people listening who you want to join you—are part of something bigger. It's not just about you; it's about what *we* can do, and how we only succeed together (or succeed separately—wait . . . I mean . . . well, you get it). Finally, the Story of Now is why this has to change immediately. What is broken? What will happen if it doesn't change? Is this a school board election that will determine the future of your children? Is it corruption in your industry that's about to spiral out of control?

The point of the framework is you get across a simple message to prospective fellow travelers: *We can do this together, and we have to do it right now.* That's your story. And by telling that story everywhere you can in every way you can, you'll attract, you'll accrue, and you'll organize.

Remember that organization I mentioned earlier called STARRS? That's *Stand Together Against Racism and Radicalism in the Services*. Their narrative compelled me to join up and support the cause. They exist in response to the problem of Cultural Marxist indoctrination through DEI and CRT at the United States military service academies. The STARRS story is this, in short: Woke ideology is destroying our ability to field effective combat teams, specifically by compromising the leadership pipeline from the service academies. The people fighting back are former officers, noncommissioned officers, and graduates of those very academies.

I was sold, immediately. The original advocates for the cause have collectivized into an organization, and I now serve on the board of advisors. STARRS was founded by Air Force Academy grads. One of them, my late friend Dennis Haugh, who wrote *The Road to Americanism*, introduced me to retired General Rod Bishop and Colonel Ron Scott. They invited me to join the board because I was already publicly working against DEI in the military, calling out how it breaks down combat readiness. That organization—STARRS—wrote the final chapter of Pete Hegseth's book *The War on Warriors*. Personally, I believe Hegseth was selected for Secretary of Defense in some large part because of their efforts. Now, they're too humble to say that, so I will. In fact, the recent executive orders dismantling DEI and removing racial quotas from service academies, STARRS proposed those policies. You can visit them at **www.STARRS.us**. These are good people who work fast. They've built teams inside West Point and the Naval Academy. They now have pathways to influence policy and legislation. It's a perfect model of Americanist organizing.

WHEN YOU CAN'T ORGANIZE, KEEP THE PEACE

Unfortunately, there will come times when we are unable to organize everyone who might otherwise support our cause. Guidelines are needed. If you understand the friend-enemy distinction, you also understand this: Don't attack your friends in public—or friends of friends. You can disagree privately, strongly even. But you do **not** go after one another publicly when you're on the same side of an issue. That makes you a divider, a tribalist, a false teacher and cult leader. So, disagreement happens behind closed doors. Speaking of cult, that's not the sort of organizing we want to be doing. If you want your movement to last beyond you and your initial momentum, think about succession and delegation. What's the chain of command? What's the plan for who leads next? How do people move up in your organization? How do you empower others to lead well? Victory has to live beyond you. This, by the way, is the only effective, practical way to keep your ego in check.

MAGA AFTER TRUMP

From a political perspective, Americanists haven't been all that successful at succession planning recently. President Ronald Reagan had a real opportunity—his was the "morning in America" movement—but it got intercepted in the 1990s by neo-conservative globalism, nation-building, and so-called "free trade." But a very real example of a quasi-political, quasi-government vision that did endure well beyond its originator was President JFK's "moonshot." His vision lived long after his death and ultimately succeeded. Seven years prior to the first moon landing, President Kennedy laid out the vision, the narrative, and the plan to make it all come to pass:

> *For the eyes of the world now look into space, to the moon and to the planets beyond, and we have vowed that we shall not see it governed by a hostile flag of conquest, but by a banner of freedom and peace. We have vowed that we shall not see space filled with weapons of mass destruction, but with instruments of knowledge and understanding.*
>
> *Yet the vows of this nation can only be fulfilled if we in this nation are first, and, therefore, we intend to be first. In short, our leadership in science and in industry, our hopes for peace and security, our obligations to ourselves as well as others, all require us to make this effort, to solve these mysteries, to solve them for the good of all men, and to become the world's leading space-faring nation.*
>
> *. . . But why, some say, the moon? Why choose this as our goal? And they may well ask why climb the highest mountain? Why, 35 years ago, fly the Atlantic? Why does Rice play Texas?*
>
> *We choose to go to the moon. We choose to go to the moon in this decade and do the other things, not because they are easy, but because they are hard, because that goal will serve to organize and measure the best of our energies and skills, because that challenge is one that we are willing to accept, one we are unwilling to postpone, and one which we intend to win, and the others, too.*

It is for these reasons that I regard the decision last year to shift our efforts in space from low to high gear as among the most important decisions that will be made during my incumbency in the office of the presidency.

. . . And this will be done in the decade of the sixties. It may be done while some of you are still here at school at this college and university. It will be done during the term of office of some of the people who sit here on this platform. But it will be done. And it will be done before the end of this decade.

I am delighted that this university is playing a part in putting a man on the moon as part of a great national effort of the United States of America.

Many years ago, the great British explorer George Mallory, who was to die on Mount Everest, was asked why did he want to climb it? He said, "Because it is there."

Well, space is there, and we're going to climb it, and the moon and the planets are there, and new hopes for knowledge and peace are there. And, therefore, as we set sail we ask God's blessing on the most hazardous and dangerous and greatest adventure on which man has ever embarked[11].

This speech gives me pause, particularly as I ponder the future of the MAGA movement. What is our organizing principle? What are we and our allies marching toward? What happens after President Trump leaves the White House? There is reason for optimism as we consider possible answers to these and other reflections. Men whom I've supported—such as Vice President JD Vance and Senator Bernie Moreno—represent the kind of leaders we will need, together with Defense Secretary Hegseth and other determined changemakers of the second Trump administration.

Still, we have to face the fact: We can't recreate Donald

---

11   John F. Kennedy, "Address at Rice University on the Nation's Space Effort," *Rice University*, September 12, 1962, https://www.rice.edu/jfk-speech.

Trump at the national level, much less local where most of us are going to be trying to make things happen. I've often reflected on my 2014 Senate race before Trump. I didn't know anything about the guy at the time—I'd never read his books; I'd just seen him on old talk shows like Phil Donahue. But looking back, the three major planks of my platform—border security, the end of endless wars, and energy independence—are what eventually helped him win. My campaign had early versions of that collective Americanist message. But I didn't have the personality, the television presence, or the unique communication skills. I've improved all of those since 2014, but no one will ever do what Trump did the way he did it.

And that's OK. What matters is building what comes next. The MAGA—or Americanism—movement is going to build a bench, with a real succession plan. It can't revolve around Trump's personality or intellect forever. The man's brilliant, but the ideas are what matter—and those ideas still resonate with **65 percent** of Americans, based on all the public polling data I've seen since 2014. That tells you something: Americanism is still alive and well and isn't going anywhere.

So, our closing question is: How do we organize around these ideas, build the bench, and create something that outlives us all? Because the machinery we're up against is powerful, and our movement is still fractured. That's not a problem for long, because this very chapter has been the solution. The two first how-to's we must adopt for the post-Trump MAGA movement are, first, organize, and second, distinguish friend versus enemy. Those two "resources" will empower what comes next. Trump is a unifying figure, no doubt about that. But when a unifying figure exits the stage, one way or another, what happens? Well, if we don't organize as well as the Left and cohere ourselves with a compelling, unifying narrative, all while rewarding our allies and punishing our enemies, we have a sense of what will happen.

Consider the fall of the Roman Empire. When the Western

Roman Emperor lost control over the various northern European tribes, local chieftains began declaring themselves kings. Europe got carved up. If you look at a map of the Roman Empire at its height versus a few centuries later, it's unrecognizable—an imperial monolith, collapsing into dozens of competing territories. That's what the Right is going to look like if we're not careful: fragmented, leaderless, disorganized. And that's exactly what will give the Left long-term dominance. Fragmentation is weakness.

After Rome fell, the greatest organized threat to the West was Islam. Not just the religion, but the highly unified and centralized force. It was ruthless in execution, intolerant of dissension, and absolutely strategic. You either submitted, or you were crushed. Coexistence wasn't an option.

The modern Left functions the same way. Their religion is DEI, BLM, gender ideology, and more. Their dogma is spoken in public confessions: "As a white person . . . " followed by apologies and affirmations of loyalty. If you don't repeat the creed-of-the-day, you're cast out. There's no tolerance. No pluralism. That's the Left. "This is what they do."

Just as Islam conquered swaths of Europe—including Spain and Portugal, among others—for hundreds of years, the modern Left will rule America, if we fracture into tiny ideological fiefdoms. If we let this movement become a map of micro-influencers and lone-wolf crusaders, they'll overrun us. So what we need going forward is this motto: *No enemies to the Right.* If someone is with us, then they're with us. We can disagree in private. But if someone is publicly attacking those on our side, they're not one of us. That's the litmus test—if you attack your own in public, you are not on the Right, period.

That said, there is one context where internal debate and criticism must be allowed—vigorous, open, and even personal— and that's during a **primary election**.

I'll admit . . . I've always struggled with this balance. On one hand, I believe in the principle of unity and no public infighting. On the other, primaries are when we sort out who's going to lead the mission. That's the time for contrast and critique. Once the primary is over, though, we close ranks. And today, with the current administration and the stakes as high as they are, I've made it a point not to criticize President Trump or his appointees in public. That doesn't mean I don't raise concerns or hold Republicans accountable, especially those in Congress who need to hear it. But I try not to fracture the movement in the process. The real challenge is figuring out the machinery—the strategies and tactics—of how we build the right team, field the right candidates, and win without tearing ourselves apart. Unity doesn't mean uniformity, and loyalty doesn't mean lying to ourselves or others. But it *does* mean knowing when and where to fight—and who the real enemy is. Sometimes, that villain lives with us. We have a name for such people: Republicans in name only, or *RINOs*. Unfortunately, a large portion of elected Republicans at every level—federal, state, and local—fall into that category. They're indistinguishable from Democrats in many ways; they're liberal Republicans, not conservative, not nationalist, not populist, not Americanist.

A lot of Republicans are allied with the enemy. They've got to go. The senators who wouldn't vote for Ed Martin for D.C. District Attorney, for example—they've made it clear they are not with us. Even if they have an "R" next to their name, they are Republicans in name only.

So, to solve the primary problem, it's not about saying "this person is an enemy because of their scandals." It's really wondering, with honest acceptance of the answer, *Who speaks best for the most of us?* It's not an attack; it's competition. Think of it like Olympic trials. Who's the best? Let the best competitor win.

Athletes go all out in the trials just like they do in the Olympics. That's the model we should follow. And we should spell that out clearly when talking about the friend/enemy distinction. Here's how you should behave in a primary: you compete. But here's where theory meets reality—in the general election: no enemies on the right. You do not publicly criticize your candidates leading up to a general election. Period.

And that means even if there's a real scandal. *What scandal? That needs to be the default. What scandal? I see no scandals here.*

When the Billy Bush tape hit during the 2016 general election, my instinct was, *Hell no, I'm not bailing. I don't care what he said on that tape—we've got our candidate. He's on the right issues.* By then, I knew he aligned with the top three issues I ran on the year before. I was all in. But RINOs like John Kennedy and Bill Cassidy ran away not like beasts of the savanna but like cockroaches when the light came on. My supporters stuck with me during my own controversy. If people had done what my supporters did, I would've won that race.

The next generation gets this. So many people experience micro-cancellations every day. They know how it feels to be ostracized for nothing, and they refuse to participate in cancel culture. It's guys who were called bigots or worse in school or college for making a simple mistake, and they're not going to join in the pile-on. They're going to defend people being canceled. That's our generation now. And especially among the online right, there's a filtering mechanism. We're crass in private. That's how we know none of us are going to fold or join the enemy's outrage mobs.

So, when we think about adopting a "no enemies to the right" stance and making that friend-enemy distinction, we do need a way to prioritize who we organize around. There are friends, good friends, and best friends—and of course the "friends in name only." Our "primary" goal must be to organize around the *best* of friends—the people who clearly, consistently speak for the 65 percent of Americans who actually believe in Americanism, by one name or another. That becomes our filter, our litmus test: ***Who speaks for the 65 percent?***

Now, who's part of the 35 percent that doesn't? Well, that group includes people who don't pay taxes, who are a net drain on the system, who operate from rent-seeking behaviors, who extract wealth through corporate grift without creating value, and who want the status quo to stay just the way it is so they can keep benefiting from it. We're not interested in organizing with or for them. We're only interested in working with the people who represent working-class and middle-class America—the builders, the doers, the people who play by the rules and contribute to this country. That's the 65 percent. So going forward, we must ask: *Who speaks best for them?* Post-Trump, as I said, that's going to be people like J.D. Vance, Bernie Moreno, and Pete Hegseth. They're the type of leaders we'll need to build around if we want the national MAGA movement to endure, grow, and win, with enthusiasm and progress that trickles right down to our own local spheres of influence.

And again one final time: *No enemies to the right.* Make the friend/enemy distinction clear. Punish the enemy, reward your friends, no matter what. That's how the Left wins, when they do. That's how you get power. And once you have power, then you can implement your principles—righteousness, justice, Americanism, and so forth. These are the things we care about but too often lack the power to make real. And you know what? As much as people love to criticize Trump, you see this behavior in him: especially after he wins. He rewards his friends and punishes his enemies. Let us go and do likewise.

What You Can Do About It

CHAPTER 10

It's Go Time

We've all heard the stories about some highly successful people that sound like this: *Wow, that guy sure was lucky. He turned a $5,000 business startup into a billion-dollar venture overnight.* Or this one: *Author so-and-so writes one book and becomes rich and famous overnight. What luck he had.*

I have to tell you another story: *Luck is made; it's not happenstance.* Luck happens for those who think, plan, and decide to work harder than anyone else in their chosen endeavor. By the way, some of you might notice that "think, plan, and decide to act" is similar to Air Force Colonel John Boyd's famous **OODA Loop**: *Observe - Orient - Decide - Act.* That shouldn't surprise us; I'm a true believer in this decision theory-turned-warfighting strategy. So much so that I keep Boyd's "Patterns of Conflict" briefing at my desk. When I was in command, I insisted that all of my officers read it. Anyway, I digress.

When I enlisted in the US Air Force three days after turning seventeen, I felt like I had finally grown up. I'd been thinking about joining the military since I was five. The planning phase took over a year—visiting recruiting offices, figuring out which specialties to ask for, and deciding on the timing to begin the work of my life as a member of America's military.

Those three initial steps—*think, plan, decide*—led to my eventual graduation from college with not one, but two degrees—in mathematics and management information systems. No one in my family had ever gone to college before, as far as I know. My education helped me navigate troubled waters when I failed out of pilot training—and yet still fly as a jet navigator and weapon systems officer, eventually commanding a combat squadron in wartime. My preparation positioned me to take advantage of special programs that led to my selection for a master's degree from Harvard University's Kennedy School—me, a kid whose parents didn't graduate from high school—and to earn two *more* master's degrees before I retired from the service.

That same foundation of *think, plan, decide* came through for me again sixteen months into my wing commander tour, when my beautiful wife Candy was diagnosed with aggressive breast cancer. Our youngest child was five years old at the time, and even though I was in a pinnacle position for a colonel in the Air Force—with a very bright future likely still ahead—I knew what needed to be done immediately. I had already been thinking and planning for retirement since making full colonel, so all I had to do was make my choice. That evening, I got in touch with my boss and friend, Major General Gary Harencak. I explained the situation and asked to retire as soon as possible to take care of Candy's treatment and our little son. He agreed.

Since part of my planning—on the advice of my mentor General Jonathan George—had included placing my résumé with a headhunter that specialized in military officer placement in civilian jobs, it wasn't more than a week before a promising opportunity came up. Within eight weeks, I had accepted an executive position with a Fortune 500 utility company in Louisiana.

The rest—my entry into the political arena and over a decade spent trying to save our Republic—is, as they say, history. And now yours has just begun.

WHAT YOU'RE GOING TO DO ABOUT IT

The Right has never had an "Organizer's Handbook" like the Left has. Again, community organizing is a Left-wing concept, and the term itself is rarely embraced by conservatives. Too often instead, the Right falls prey to "outrage pornography." It's political news and opinion that make us feel intense emotions in the moment— anger, betrayal, indignation—but nothing lasting comes from it. There's no follow-up, no organizing, no strategic spreading of effort or influence. Just a high followed by a crash. All that's left is a mess. Nothing actually happened. No policy changed. No power was gained. No real-world consequence. Conservatives have been unable to successfully reproduce the culture—or any of the mainstream institutions.

We the people have had enough of that now. There's a New Right emerging, very different from the old guard GOP and the large conservative businesses we collectively call "Con, Inc."

Con, Inc.'s contribution is basically, *Look at those liberals being liberal. They're liberalizing everything. Everything's liberal now. OK, back after our commercial break—we're going to talk about more liberals!* It's not even reactionary. It's just complaining. Or more accurately, *whining.* Then they pitch their mug, their tumbler, their T-shirt, their pillowcase, and tell you to come back tomorrow for more. *Oh, and be sure to catch the latter half of the episode. We've got a premium subscription special: 10% off your first month with code "AMERICA."* That's Con, Inc.

The fecklessness of Con, Inc. is why I get asked all the time, "Rob, what can I do about it?" People never get any real meat from status-quo Right-wingers. We're not given a way to dive in and actually do our part to build and perpetuate the culture or the movement. That's why this book exists, among others. It's not just another round of conservative complaints about what the Left is doing. We're realizing—especially in these early days of the 47th presidency, at the time of this writing—that it's not enough just to win the presidency. If your own party in the Senate or House refuses to cooperate, nothing gets done.

Change can't be top-down. It *has* to be bottom-up. Not just through corporations or national movements or even state-level coalitions but all the way down to individuals like you, reading this book right now.

The thing that matters to you, the thing you want to change right now . . . that's what matters **most**. Most of us aren't trying to become president or senator with zero experience leading a team. Most of us aren't retired military officers. Most of you are regular people—like soccer moms and little league dads. That's where meaningful, lasting input and change happen.

Now, that said, the unexpected lesson about what you can do about it—the very title of this book—is that it's not simply about *what* you can do. It's about *who* you must become in order to be capable of doing something about it. Whatever the "it" is for you, and whatever you're upset about, that anger is your fuel. It can be transformed—alchemically, you could say—into **purpose-driven action**. It doesn't need to feed more outrage for outrage's sake. Instead, it can stoke meaningful change. And it's OK—even *healthy*—that the pain of staying the same has finally become greater than the pain of doing something. It's helpful to feel negative emotions about what's happening under your watch—in your industry, your school district, your library system, your neighborhood, your culture, your street, even your home. Whatever's in your backyard that feels intolerable . . . it's time.

Even Jesus Christ, when he saw institutionalized corruption

in the temple—where poor Jewish worshippers were being extorted—didn't retreat into spiritual detachment or find some meditative practice to "process" his emotional "trauma." Nope, he cracked a whip and started flipping tables. He took swift, decisive action. And what fueled him? *Righteous anger.* It wasn't sinful; it was just and right.

So what's your version of that money-changers-in-the-temple moment? Of all the things that frustrate or anger you, what's the **one thing** that makes your blood boil—so much so that to allow it would feel like endorsing it? That's your thing; that's what you need to act on.

The Left gets this part right, even if they misapply it. They like to say, "Silence is violence." And while we might phrase it differently—perhaps "Silence is compliance."—the point stands. If you don't do something, others will interpret your inaction as acceptance. They'll say, "Well, if they're not stopping it, maybe we should go along with it." But when you stand up and say *no*—metaphorically grabbing your whip, flipping those proverbial tables—that act sets a new standard. You create a permission structure for others to say no, too, in word and deed.

Now, don't forget what Jesus said after his act of defiance. He didn't rage and leave. He laid out a vision, which I'll paraphrase: "My Father's house is a house of prayer, but you have made it a den of thieves." Notice the direction, the vision-casting. Jesus made clear what the standard should be (house of prayer) and what must no longer be tolerated (den of thieves).

So, what is your one-sentence vision? In three to five words, or one strong sentence, what are you building? What are you calling into existence? What will this thing look like when it's right? And who needs to hear it? Who are your people? You may come up with your vision in private, but the next step is to make it known—publicly, boldly, clearly. Again, not just what you're against. That's the Con, Inc. trap—to keep people endlessly angry so they'll buy another subscription, another branded product, another advertiser-approved purchase. You're not here to money-change outrage; you're here to rebuild America.

Now, the one thing that drove me to enter the political arena as a candidate was the endless war policies. Yes, I was a senior officer; I was in the 1 to 2 percent who earned command multiple times. I fought in those wars. So someone like me had to stand up and take that policy on—and I did, in my US Senate races. Endless war was one of my top three issues, even though I caught a lot of heat for it—figuratively and literally—from colleagues. But that was my flipping-the-tables moment. I was one of the few who could, so I had to.

As for my vision, what's the opposite of "no more endless wars"? In just a few words, it's **peace through strength**. That was the message of my campaigns. And though I didn't win elected office, I brought national attention to that issue as early as 2014. Ultimately, that message became a defining plank of the Trump administration. And now, even though I'm not in office, I continue to remind local, state, and federal Republican leaders that peace through strength is still one of the most important policy positions a candidate can take.

Just recently, when President Donald Trump spoke in the Middle East, a clip of him went viral. In that speech, he verbally whipped neoconservative, nation-building policy and called for its end. Basically that it's time to get the hell out of other people's countries and let them run their own affairs. That was the message I started sharing ten years earlier—and now it's our nation's geopolitical policy. Here are my favorite excerpts from that special speech.

- "This great transformation has not come from Western interventionists … giving you lectures on how to live or how to govern your own affairs. No, the gleaming marvels of Riyadh and Abu Dhabi were not created by the so-called 'nation-builders,' 'neo-cons,' or 'liberal non-profits,' like those who spent trillions failing to develop Kabul and Baghdad, so many other cities. Instead, the birth of a modern Middle East has been brought about by the people of the region themselves … developing your own sovereign countries, pursuing your own unique visions, and charting your own destinies[12]."

- "In the end, the so-called 'nation-builders' wrecked far more nations than they built — and the interventionists were intervening in complex societies that they did not even understand themselves[13]."

- "After so many decades of conflict, finally it is within our grasp to reach the future that generations before us could only dream about — a land of peace, safety, harmony, opportunity, innovation, and achievement right here in the Middle East[14]."

- "As I have shown repeatedly, I am willing to end past conflicts and forge new partnerships for a better and more stable world, even if our differences may be very profound[15]."

- "In recent years, far too many American presidents have been afflicted with the notion that it's our job to look into the souls of foreign leaders and use U.S. policy to dispense justice for their sins … I believe

---

12   Rapid Response 47 (@RapidResponse47), "Post," *X (formerly Twitter)*, May 2026, https://x.com/RapidResponse47/status/1922322254622343286
13   Ibid.
14   Rapid Response 47 (@RapidResponse47), "Post," *X (formerly Twitter)*, May 2026, https://x.com/RapidResponse47/status/1922320579098501198
15   Rapid Response 47 (@RapidResponse47), "Post" *X (formerly Twitter)*, May 2025, https://x.com/RapidResponse47/status/192232321082778024

> it is God's job to sit in judgement — my job [is] to
> defend America and to promote the fundamental
> interests of stability, prosperity, and peace[16]."

That's the indirect yet meaningful influence a person can have, even without a title or office. If I hadn't recognized that I was one of the people who could speak out—and should speak out—that message might never have caught on. But I knew it had to be me. For those reading this, as you begin your journey to do something about "it," you'll also find that there are people in your life—mentors, family, historical figures—who will become your models. Some are close to you. Others are larger-than-life icons who you admire and want to emulate.

But here's what you need to understand: The first pitfall you'll encounter on this journey isn't the opposition; it's yourself. It's your lack of awareness, your blind spots, your naïveté, or your weaknesses that could be exploited. You need to either deal with those flaws now or decide that they won't stop you. That you don't care. That you will not apologize, no matter what.

Look at Donald Trump again. The Woman Question followed him in all three presidential elections, even through the final weeks of the 2024 campaign. But he never apologized. He never appeared ashamed or embarrassed. He just said, in effect, "Who cares? Bill Clinton was worse, and you loved him." That was exactly my response when the Billy Bush tape hit in 2016. I was running for Senate again, and the media came to me asking what I thought. My answer? Two words: Bill Clinton.

Look, the media don't care about women; they care about damaging Republicans. I knew it. Trump knew it. And he made a choice—a choice you must make, too: Either clean up your

---

16   Rapid Response 47 (@RapidResponse47), "Post," *X (formerly Twitter)*, May 2026, https://x.com/RapidResponse47/status/1922325565987537046

vulnerabilities now, or accept that they exist and decide that you will never apologize. No matter what they drag out from your past, you will not play their game. That's the decision you make now, before anything happens—before the smear campaigns begin, before the hit pieces, before the whisper networks light up. Because if you're serious about becoming a public power player, you'll face all of that. You have to either completely guarantee it will never come out, or you have to bring it out yourself and neutralize it as an attack.

Never lie. Never apologize. There may be skeletons in your closet, so you either need to bury them in concrete in the middle of nowhere or drag them out, dress them up, and make a show of it all to take that attack vector away.

Beyond neutralizing your vulnerabilities, you also need to develop strengths you don't currently have. Scott Adams calls this building your "talent stack." These are the things that, when added together, make you formidable. For most people, that means a thick skin, a sense of humor, edge thinking, and nonconformity. If you're going to lead people, you need to be a confident public speaker—not someone who's monotone or afraid to show up. You should be able to give a speech to two people like it's an audience of a thousand. And you should be able to talk to a thousand people like you're chatting with your spouse. Both are essential.

That's going to take practice. And there's something else, too—a frustration a lot of people on the right have. It's the gatekeeping. The cash-money fiefdoms. The ecosystem of pollsters, pundits, the writers, the influencers . . . all the people who control the conversation and guard access to influence. They make a living off of being conservative. It's a brand for them. They've got their audiences, their subscriptions, their email lists, their merch—selling mugs, t-shirts, premium content. It's not a movement. It's a monetized live-action roleplay. At some point, instead of having an audience, the audience has *you*. You stop taking risks. You stop being bold. But for you, if you're going to build something—an organization, a campaign, a for-profit company, a movement—you are going to need resources. And your work can be leveraged by others, just like mine was. My campaign messaging became national policy a decade later.

Your job is to reward your friends. Spend your energy fighting your enemies. That's it.

All of this leads to this point right now. *It's go time.*

First thing you need: your three-to-five-word vision statement. This is your foundation. What do you want? What are you trying to build? Then, share it with two or three people. Remember what the Bible says: where two or three are gathered, I am with them. There is power in agreement, in unity. Share your vision with others and begin building. Organize. Go.

But if you're worried about skeletons in your closet, about shame, or cancellation . . . don't worry. I invite you to join my email list; I have a special chapter just for you, a bonus Chapter 11. It's entitled "How to Cancel Your Own Cancellation." This will fortify your courage, protect your reputation, and let you make progress in your work as quickly as you want—not as slowly as the opposition media allows.

Read it for free at www.robmaness.com/bonus-chapter.

See you in Chapter 11!

9/11 After Action Report

One week after the September 11th, 2001, terrorist attacks on United States citizens, military personnel, and infrastructure, I wrote a now-unclassified after action report. No changes have been made to the original text.

I've included this report in *What You Can Do About It* to show the necessity of the first stage of the OODA loop—observe, orient, decide, and act. Before you can respond in a crisis or create great and lasting change, *you need to know what the hell is going on*. And that's the purpose of this report in the context of the impending Global War On Terror (GWOT). Let this be a lesson.

One final note: You'll read about a man named Brian in the report. That's Brian Birdwell, a Texas State Senator as of this writing. But on that day in 2001, I thought Brian, given his severe injuries, was a goner. Destiny had another plan. From a 2016 *People* magazine article:

Every day for almost 15 years, Col. Rob Maness wondered about the badly-burned man he'd tried to keep conscious on a gurney after terrorists flew a 757 airliner into the Pentagon on Sept. 11, 2001.

Did he make it? Was he still alive? Was he able to fully recover and live a happy and fulfilling life?

. . . Last week, while attending the Republican National Convention in Cleveland, Maness, now retired from the Air Force, was told that former Texas governor Rick Perry wanted to meet with him and several other veterans.

After shaking Maness' hand, Gov. Perry told him, "Rob, I want you to meet somebody. He was in the Pentagon on 9/11, too."

The governor introduced him to Brian Birdwell, a state senator from Granbury, Texas, who had been severely burned on the right side of his body in the attack and required 39 surgeries.

As Birdwell, 54, relayed his story and mentioned that a stranger had helped hold his IV line and talked to him while he was waiting to be transported to a hospital, Maness knew: This was the man he had thought about daily since that horrific morning when American Airlines Flight 77 crashed into the Pentagon.

"When I realized that I was looking at the same gentleman, I started to cry and told him I was so grateful that he was still alive," Maness tells PEOPLE. "We hugged each other and neither of us could believe that we were talking again. What are the odds[17]?"

What are the odds indeed.

Here now is my after action report, preceded by a **diagram** of the affected areas of the Pentagon and surrounding area on 9/11.

---

17   Cathy Free, "Nearly 15 Years After 9/11, Retired Colonel Meets the Man Whose Life He Helped Save," *People*, July 25, 2016, https://people.com/celebrity/911-anniversary-retired-colonel-meets-man-he-helped-save/

The explosion graphic and arrow indicate the airline's point of impact and direction upon collision into the Pentagon. The star graphic at the tip of the arrow is the location where I and others worked in an attempt to put out the fire and search for the wounded. The star graphic to the right of that is my original location that morning inside the National Military Command Center when the airplane crashed into the Pentagon. The most eastern star on the illustration was the ensuing medical triage area outside.

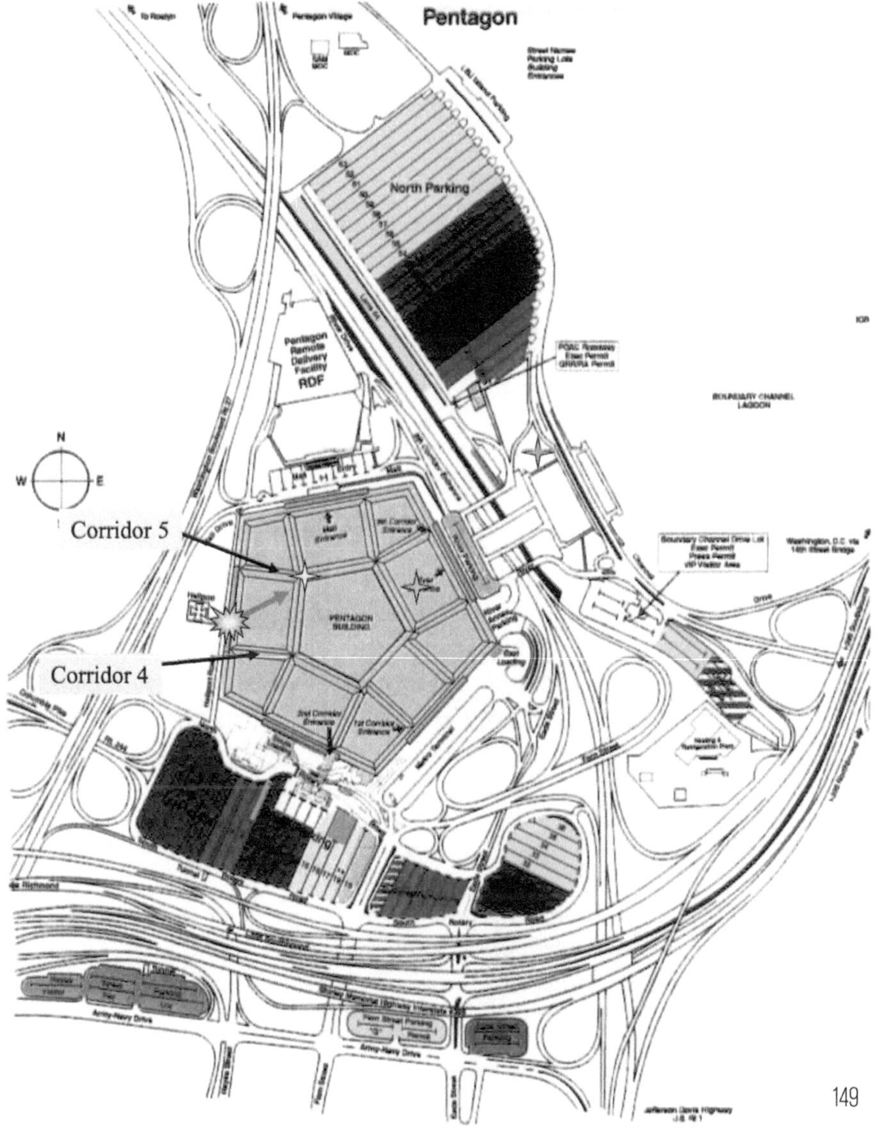

Maness, Robert L., Maj, NMCC

From: Maness, Robert L., Maj, NMCC

Sent: 18 September 2001 12:47 PM

To: OSD-C3I

Subject: SEP 11 After Action Report

Importance: High

CLASSIFICATION: UNCLASSIFIED

I thought I would write down my recollections and observations of the events of 11 Sep. Maybe there are some lessons someone can learn from them.

11 Sep at approximately 8;30 am.

I heard about the first WTC first tower while on the phone with a colleague in Europe. I got off the phone and went to find a television.

Watched second aircraft crash into second WTC tower a few minutes later.

Heard reports of another crash on Interstate 395 south of the Pentagon.

I immediately called my wife (she works in the Army Times building in Springfield) and told her to go home and stay off the interstate) 0945 - Pentagon under attack... first evacuation call....I went over to front office to see if I could help CDR Ling who is standing in as EA for Grif...he asked me to help him make sure the Division's offices were empty...after checking all the offices I went back to check in with him.

1000 - Col Matthews (the Admiral's Deputy) ordered me out and I proceeded to the River Entrance exit on the second floor right next to the Chairman of the Joint Chief's Office (General Hugh Shelton) Exited at River Entrance...all was calm (no one's around the area except the Chairman's security detail) until I reached the end of the grass area (field in front of River Entrance that extends almost to Boundary Channel Drive...100 yards or so... proceeded down the North steps toward Boundary Channel Drive...as I walked away from the building I looked back at the building to check the damage and wind direction I observed dense black smoke billowing above me and toward the southeast... this against a backdrop of crystal-clear blue skies.

Continued down the steps on the North side of the grassy area toward the North Parking area. At the bottom of the hill I looked back up toward the Pentagon Officer's Athletic Club (POAC) entrance and spotted an old friend of mine (Maj Soren Jones, USAF) directing people down the hill...I noticed that most of the people who evacuated the building were gathered across Boundary Channel by the water away from the building (huge crowd of several thousand people).

Decided to go up toward the building where Soren was and see if I could help.

When I got to him we started seeing the first casualties come out so he moved further up on the POAC bridge to Corridor 8 entrance while I took up his position and started directing casualties down to the bottom of the hill where I now noticed the medics from the clinic were trying to set up a triage area At first the casualties were walking wounded (about 5 or 6 of them) but then folks started coming out being carried and on stretchers in pretty bad shape (burns, both legs broken, trouble breathing types of injuries). I had to leave my post to help assist a Navy Petty Officer (PO) down to the medics area (I lost track of Soren at this time)

After getting the PO to the medics I started back up the hill to my position for directing casualties. As I reached my old position I met a couple of guys transporting a severely injured Army Officer out of the building on a gurney. We had to get medics up the hill to take a look at this guy and call for an ambulance, so one of the transporters asked me to hold the IV bags on a for him while he ran down to get a medic or doctor while we continued slowly down the hill toward the triage area. (I soon realized there were no ambulances or medevac helicopters to be seen even though all hell was breaking loose and the medics appeared to be getting overwhelmed)

The Army Officer's IV line was broken so as we continued getting him down the hill I closed off the line and held it until we could get a medic to replace it at the bottom of the hill. We began to ask about transporting this guy (his name was Brian and he had burns, lacerations, fractures in the legs (I think) and was in Shock. No one was coming to get a new IV in this guy so when an AF Chaplain came up I had him hold the line closed I went to the medic's triage area (about 20 yards away) to find a new IV line and get someone to put it in (as I said this guy was in shock and for some reason I was worried contamination or air would get into his bloodstream if we didn't get the IV taken care of), also needed to get the only Doctor (right now an Army Capt) in sight over to check him out and get transport secured using his communications gear.

Just as I was walking over to find a Dr and IV line we started getting warnings of another air attack. The large crowd of evacuees split in two and headed for the overpasses (at each end of Boundary) while we were still working the casualties.

Things really got confusing right about now...I successfully got the Doc to go over to this badly injured guy with the busted IV line then went in search of the line and a tech to fix it.

About the time I succeeded in medic with a new IV line we began to move patients across Boundary Channel and under the trees so they couldn't be seen from the air. I also remember going back up the hill toward the building to warn Maj Jones (I thought he was at the Corridor 8 entrance) but instead I ran into another group of volunteers bringing a gurney out with a critical patient on it.

They asked me where to go fro a medevac helicopter so I warned them of the impending attack and directed them to go to the far end of the area we had selected for a landing area (the grass area in between the Pentagon Flags along Boundary Channel Drive) which also would provide them some cover with its 6 foot high concrete wall. I went back to helping move patients across the road and ran into my old navigator training flight commander when I helped him move a casualty across the street (Col Cox, USAF retired). All the while several more medics and more volunteer help was arriving and we (myself and a couple of others continued to press medics with radios for medevac helicopters and ambulances.

An AF Lt Col (female) took charge (myself and a couple of civilians assisted her with dispersal efforts) of getting hazardous material (6 large Oxygen tanks had been piled together within 5 feet of the medical aid area) and the patients were dispersed so we didn't all get killed by exploding tanks if the area was hit by this second attack while the rest of us were dealing with getting more casualties down the hill and treated by medics (also continuing to work to get transport).

A couple of ambulances finally showed up and the medics started loading patients. The issue of medevac helicopters and the right location to land them came up again when a nurse asked me where the best place was. I again indicated the grass area in between the flagpoles on the Pentagon side of the road would be the best place. Unfortunately we still had no comms connectivity with airborne assets. (We got sight of the first combat air patrol jet about this time...I felt a lot more comfortable and so did a lot of others)

Right after the jet went over a medic from inside an ambulance yelled at me to help him pull a female patient out that wasn't able to travel by road and would need the dust off so we replaced her with another, more suitable patient. At this time I noticed an AF 2-star medical officer (who had been inside the building getting casualties out) showed up and things began to be a little better organized from the medical perspective.

We finally got all the patients settled and either on ground transport or awaiting the medevac helo arrival and the next thing we knew the general was asking for volunteers to go inside to the courtyard and pull casualties from the impact area from that side. We organized ourselves into 3 teams of about 15 or 20 people proceeded inside the building through Corridor 8). We used our T-shirts (always wondered why we wore those now I know) soaked with water from the latrine just inside the Corridor 8 entrance for respiratory protection. The smoke and heat in corridor 8 was building as we entered from the North side of the building so we did need it. We marched single file through the smoke down Corridor 8 and into the courtyard.

Our team was in the lead as we arrived inside courtyard. As we prepared to enter the Pentagon through the Corridor 3/4 entrance fire fighters emerged.

Smoke, heat, and flames emanated from the doors and it certainly didn't appear likely that we could get through that way. The fire fighters pushed us back toward the courtyard area and briefed the team leader that we would have to try the corridor 5/6 entrance on the other side of the impact area or wait. The AF 2-star decided to keep our team out in the courtyard and organize it as a triage element.

Observed another team approach the corridor 3/4 entrance and prepare to enter so moved to new team picked up back end of a stretcher, (AF/PA BG Rand had the other end it turned out) but we were stopped by fire fighters again.

General Rand and I moved over to the corridor 5/6 courtyard entrance when we noticed another team of volunteers was going inside. Got inside up to the B and C ring alleyway between corridor 5 and 4. The attack impact point was in between corridors 4 and 5. We were now about 50 feet north of where the American Airlines jet's travel had stopped, just breaking through the inner wall of the C-ring and spilling burning debris into the alley way between B and C rings.

We had not seen anyone but other volunteers and firemen to this point.

*As I was checking out the aircraft debris and damage I o
bserved through the smoke, flames and water spray the
On-scene commander (a volunteer named, Lt Col Kaiser,
USMC, who's office happened to be closed to the impact
point) directing the effort to extinguish the fire emanating
from the breach in the C ring wall. A volunteer named
CAPT Lamme US Army, and a volunteer AF Chief Master
Sgt (CMSgt) briefed us in preparation to enter through
corridor 5 and search for wounded.*

*The fire flared up and forced us back out to courtyard. We
did this drill a couple of times and finally we stayed in the
courtyard in order to wait for the fire to ease up so we could
get in the building safely. The team leader, a physician, was
called away when all medically trained personnel were
summoned so I took over as the team leader.*

*For the next few hours I coordinated between the On-
scene-commander (inside the B and C ring alley way)
and the search team members. Security personnel and I
established a classified material collection point at the
entry to Corridor 5/6 (lots of classified was blowing around
from where the aircraft had traveled through the E, D, and
C Rings). I also began debriefing fire fighting teams and
reporting my findings to the National Military Command
Center (Gen Shelton had sent someone down to get status
earlier) from the hard-line phone at the Corridor 5/6
entrance.)*

*As I was working to coordinate our efforts I also helped
survey the damage by assisting the CMSgt working the
inside with identifying aircraft parts, remains etc.*

*He eventually got FBI agents in to start collecting evidence.
There were several more attempts to get searchers inside
but the fire and smoke were just too intense and the
fire fighters couldn't get it under control so we backed
volunteers out each time.*

*At about 3;30 pm The On Scene Commander outside (on the
West side of the building) finally made a decision to begin
the search from the outside in instead of from inside out so*

Lt Col Kaiser led the team out to the staging area on HWY 27 (just West of the Helo pad) to prepare for that. (I phoned in a situation report to CDR Pat Gardner in the Deputy Director for Operations shack inside the national military commander center prior to leaving my post so he would know we no longer had volunteer search team manpower available in the courtyard)

Finally, after waiting with about 300 other volunteers I realized that nobody from our group was going to get in the impact area (and there were probably no survivors to pull out) until the fire was under control and that would definitely be the next day, decided to go to my vehicle (walked to North parking) and where I got on the cell phone to contact my family. I also called and checked in with my boss who directed me to go home and stay there until called.

Unfortunately, from the time we helped the casualties out in the North area on Boundary Channel Drive, we didn't see any more survivors the rest of the day.

V/R

Rob

Robert L. Maness, Maj, USAF

JCS J-38 NOD-NOB

DSN227-9169

Acknowledgments

First and foremost, I would like to express my appreciation for my grandchildren, who have learned and are indeed re-teaching me the price of our liberty—eternal vigilance. I love you all.

We stand on the shoulders of giants. This is true, too, of authors. Those who have come before me and alongside me include dear family and distinguished friends. With a grateful heart, I would like to thank:

> My Mom, Lennie R. Maness, and Dad, retired Air Force MSgt Billy J. Maness (Western Tennessee), for providing us the most exciting adventures we could have ever hoped for around the world.

> My wife Candy, the foundation of our family, for getting on board the crazy ride of life with me and staying on!

> My Aunts and Uncles, who taught me to study and honor my heritage.

> My children, who love and support me despite my many flaws and mistakes.

> My EOD School Marines, Lt. Benjamin O. Bell, Sgt. Garcia, and Gunner (Warrant Officer) Weigh.

> My Air Force Dad, retired EOD Senior Master Sergeant Jim Powlas (North Carolina).

> Governor Sarah Palin (Alaska).

> Lt. Governor Billy Nungesser (Louisiana).

My loyal political campaign teammates, including
Strategist Jason Recher, Campaign Managers Mike
Byrne and Andy Surabian, fundraisers Loren Bosler,
Krista Carter, and Jay Rao.

Former Sirius XM Radio host and current terrestrial
Radio Host, friend, and neighbor Mike Church.

Stephen K. Bannon, who put me on the national
conservative stage through his Sirius XM Radio show,
and who has led the America First movement.

My loyal Louisiana friends who taught me grassroots
organizing and TEA Party politics: Kelly Camp, Sarah
Wood, Mary Kass, Candy Peavy, Flight Doc (US Navy)
and oil company executive Pat Peavy.

Air Force Academy graduates Dennis Haugh, retired Lt
Gen Rod Bishop, and retired Colonel Ron Scott. Dennis
for his service and his authorship of books like The
Road To Americanism, reminding me of what I am, an
Americanist, and for connecting me to General Bishop
and Colonel Scott, who are the amazing men behind
Stand Together Against Racism and Radicalism in the
Services, STARRS.US[18].

The 231 courageous American servicemembers,
veterans, and one military spouse who signed the
Declaration of Military Accountability.

Soldier and Sailor Shawn Cronan, I know you're
looking down on all this and thank you for challenging
me to enter the political arena to continue my service.

---

18   Stand Together Against Racism and Radicalism in the Services (STARRS), "About,"
      STARRS, accessed April 21, 2026, http://starrs.us.

General Ron Fogelman for sending me to Officer Training School.

Master Sergeant Junior Ladd, for lobbying the boss (Fogelman) to support my OTS application.

Brigadier General Jonathan George and Colonel Jack Wiley, Air Force commanders who had enough faith in me to push hard for a prior enlisted navigator to command at every level.

The men and women of the Bone (B-1B) aircrews and maintenance, especially my 9th Bomb Squadron Bats, who accomplished every mission we were ever tasked with and get all the credit, from the Best Bomber crew in the entire Air Force to the squadron winning Commander-in-Chief award recognition.

The men and women of the Fighting 55th Wing, America's airborne intelligence wing, who've been deployed continuously to the Middle East since Desert Shield and Desert Storm and operate our most challenging missions, like the Rivet Joint, Cobra Ball, the DoomsDay aircraft (national Airborne Operations Center) and Nuclear Sniffing intelligence aircraft (Constant Phoenix).

The men and women of the 377th Air Base Wing: You were and are the Tigers we envisioned together enabling and accomplishing our Nation's most vital missions: national laboratories, nuclear deterrence, and all those I can't mention for classification reasons.

The men and women of J-38 nuclear operations 1999-2002 . . . you know what you did (highly classified) for our country, and I am grateful and humbled to have been a small part of it.

Finally, the two individuals who came into my life totally by accident who made it possible for me to do this book: my friends Joshua Lisec and Jack Posobiec. And Joshua, I am proud to know you—and am honored to be your number 100.

Thank you, everyone. Thank you.

About the Author

Col. Robert L. Maness, ret. is a decorated combat veteran and dynamic leader with over forty years of experience steering complex organizations through high-stakes challenges. A retired U.S. Air Force Colonel with thirty-two years of service, Maness has an unmatched track record of turning around failing systems, building high-performing teams, and delivering results under pressure—whether in war zones, corporate boardrooms, or political arenas. During his military service, Maness received eighteen major awards and decorations, including the Legion of Merit twice and a Bronze Star for combat leadership.

Maness' 2013-2014 U.S. Senate run on "America First" principles rallied 210,000 votes, while his GatorPAC has brought millions of donor dollars into like-minded candidates such as JD Vance and Donald J. Trump. He is the first of his family to graduate from college, with master's degrees from the Naval War College and Harvard University. Maness is also a small business owner who has even owned a small farm and host of The Rob Maness Show. Watch live Monday through Friday every week at www.robmaness.com.

FREE CONTENT UPGRADE

Want more?
Get your free bonus chapter at
www.robmaness.com/bonus-chapter

It's a direct extension of what you've just read—practical,
unfiltered, and worth your time.